ADVENTURE WITH A PURPOSE

ADVENTURE WITH A PURPOSE

"12 Trail Tested Elements of Adventure"

JACK WARD

Adventure with a Purpose, 12 Trail-Tested Elements of Adventure
Copyright 2017 by Jack Ward

ISBN: 0692825533
ISBN 9780692825532
Published by Rugged Faith Publishers
3907 Shannendoah Lane
Springdale, AR 72762
www.ruggedfaith.net

Cover design by
Lamb Creek Design
1207 Monroe Drive
Kerrville, TX78028

First Printing 2017
Printed by Create Space in the United States

TABLE OF CONTENTS

INTRODUCTION

"Every path has its purpose"

KATE CLOW

I HAVE ALWAYS HAD the urge to wander, to see new places, meet interesting people, and experience different things. I think I caught the adventure bug from my dad.

Woods wise and stream smart; my dad was a great outdoorsman. He could find and kill wild game like nobody I've ever known.

He could paddle a riverboat up and down the White River with ease. He could follow bees to their hives inside a hollow tree and steal their wild honey. He could sharpen a knife, carve a whistle out of a hickory branch, build rabbit snares, and call wild turkey with a reed.

He was a tracker, a gatherer of wild editable plants, and he was a survivor who had spent four long years on the islands of the Pacific during WWII.

This book is a call to adventure. A call especially to Christian men, who sometimes feel trapped in their jobs, and family responsibilities, yet yearn for periods of adventure. This work is not an attempt to "spiritualize" adventure, but to make you more aware of the benefits of adventure in every area of your life.

The story line for this book details a recent trip to Israel to hike the Jesus Trail, a forty-mile trail that stretches from Nazareth to the Sea of Galilee, plus other exciting stories of adventure, exploration, and various expeditions.

What I experienced along the Jesus Trail was certainly colored and enriched by my travel companions. If not for my friends Dale Armstrong, Jim Zalenski, Bill Hoffman, and Mike Howell, the trip and this book would not have been possible.

The book is infused with the good news of Jesus Christ. You will find the Gospel runs deep; it's not a shallow, murky message, but a deep, and clear, life-giving message.

We will also look at twelve elements of adventure. Each chapter will focus on a different element. Elements such as perseverance, courage, impact, creating memories, and finding direction. Each chapter ends with a "Trail Thought," a question or challenge to help you get the most out of each chapter.

Each chapter has a three-prong focus I call "MAT" <u>Ministry</u> related topics, <u>Adventure</u> based stories, and <u>Trail</u> stories from my time in Israel. The chapters are also subdivided into easy to follow segments.

Alastair Humphreys reminds us, "There is often a perception that adventure is for "Adventurers" rather than "normal people." I know better than anyone that adventures are not all tough, brave and special. We are ordinary people who just make the choice to do things that are not so ordinary."

Those "Oh My God" moments keep us searching for the next breath-taking vista, the urge to go, the wanderlust is inside a man. In the 1970's classic adventure book Deliverance, one of the characters describes adventures this way, "They tell me that this is the kind of thing that gets hold of middle-class householders every once-in-a-while. But most of them just lie down till the feeling passes."

Today's man needs adventure, we need an escape from the mundane of daily routine and periods of adventure can be an oasis in the desert of dull sameness. Adventure can be a pathway to purpose.

My friend Jim Zalenksi says, "Men today have ADD, Adventure Deficit Disorder." The symptoms include fatigue, restlessness, boredom, stress, thirst, hunger, the constant need to go, farsightedness, and a constant itch.

One of my favorite poets is Robert Service. In his classic, gritty work "The Lone Trail" he speaks of a man's call to adventure.

> "The trails of the world would be countless
> And most of the trails be tried
> You tread on the heels of the many
> Till you come where the ways divide
> Yet you look aslant at the Lone Trail
> And the Lone Trail lures you on."

Special thanks to the following people who have made Rugged Faith Ministries possible; My wonderful wife Brenda Ward, Jim Zalenski, Steve Perryman, Brian Center, Jeff Boyd, Rusty Jones, Michael Brown, Gerald Johnson, Mike Graen, John Miles, and Mel Reed who have served on our Board of Directors and offered valuable support. Others like Charles Walden, Michael Brewer, Grant Rowell, John Greenler, Jim Greenslade, Dale Armstrong, Jim Shaw, and Wes George have advised and served to advance our ministry to men.

1

On the Trail ...Perseverance

RUGGED FAITH IS a tough, never quit attitude that pushes us to know God better. I have found that both faith and adventure require perseverance, which can be defined as steadfastness in doing something despite the difficulty in achieving the goal. The greatest predictor of success for any adventure is your tolerance for adversity. In this chapter, we will focus on the virtue of perseverance as we explore the Jesus Trail in Israel.

The trail ahead was steep and rocky. I adjusted my Gregory backpack, which was beginning to feel like 128 pounds instead of its actual 28 pounds. The blisters on my feet were becoming near unbearable with each step. My breathing was labored and fast. My shoulders ached, my throat was dry and my mind was saying stop and rest.

Despite the sweat and pain, I'm smiling. I'm smiling because we were hiking the Jesus Trail in northern Israel, 40 miles of dirt paths, rocky roads, and steep village streets that stretch from Nazareth to the Sea of Galilee.

It was November 2011. I had joined four friends on a 14-day trip to Israel; the Promised Land, the place where Jesus walked. What could be more exciting for a Christian who loves the outdoors?

Six months earlier my friend Dale Armstrong had invited me to join him and a few other guys for this trip. It took me about three seconds to accept his kind offer. Armed with a lot of excitement and a backpack full of questions I began to prepare for this adventure with the purpose of getting to know God better.

WHY MEN NEED ADVENTURE

Why would men put themselves through intense physical pain and mental anguish in order to be part of an outdoor adventure? We will give up time with family, put off important projects, travel thousands of miles, spend hundreds of hours training, and devote thousands of dollars of hard-earned money, to experience pain that most people try to avoid.

I think it all goes the back to creation. God created men with an adventurous spirit, with a deep yearning to explore, to strike out, and too see what's over the next hill. Author John Eldredge says, "There is something in every man that was wired for adventure from boyhood."

Perhaps it's the warrior inside a man that pushes us, or maybe it's the fact that our modern workday does not provide, for most men, the adrenaline rush we so desperately need. David Murrow points out that In the Great Commission found in Matthew 28 we find that "Jesus left us a dangerous and demanding mission, a great adventure."

The word adventure is defined as, "an unusual and exciting, sometimes hazardous, experience or activity." In our mundane work-day, the unusual and exciting are rare. Adventure can be painful, but the mundane can destroy a man's soul.

The words <u>advent</u> and <u>adventure</u> have the same Latin root, meaning, "about to happen." Advent refers to the days leading up to the coming of Christ at Christmas, while adventure is the expectation of coming excitement.

Men need adventure. Men need the excitement and a challenge of something big. Adventure provides something to look forward to and something to train for. George Eliot once said, "Adventure is not outside man, it's within."

Looking forward to what lies ahead. Great expectations of things to come; these are the fuel that power men through the mundane. In the book "Deliverance," the Burt Reynolds character is described this way, "In his mind Lewis was always leaving, always going somewhere, always doing something else."

Someone once said, "The currency of life isn't in dollars, it's in time and experiences. We should aim to fill our lives with adrenalin and with rich experiences." Today, meaning is the new money and purpose pays dividends. A life without adventure is of little value. I meet many men who would gladly exchange a reduced salary for more time, freedom, and purpose in life. Many find more purpose in life from adventure than from money. Chuck Colson one said, "Human life is characterized by divine restlessness. The lack of peace within a man's heart spurs him on to a quest for meaning and purpose."

All of us have had trouble sleeping the night before a road trip or the beginning of a planned expedition. We are all packed, we have put in hours of training to get ready, and the time can't arrive soon enough. Like kids on Christmas morning, we are up before the sun.

As I write this, I glance at my notes from that day in 2011. I had written the following, "Left home full of excitement, eager to begin after weeks of anticipation. Lord what do you want to teach me on this trip?"

Even after six decades of life I still find myself nervously anticipating any upcoming adventure. So many seniors I know retire early in life only to be bored and unfulfilled. I want to avoid those feeling. Life is too interesting to fall into that mindset.

I sometimes feel like we need to issue a "Silver Alert" for those folks who have so much to offer if only they would get in the game. Several times my pastor has reminded me, "It's too soon to quit."

Armchair adventurers watching Bear Grylls on TV is not that same as experience gained in the wild. Its through adventure and meaningful work accomplishments we forge memories which are the storehouse of stories we can draw from for years to come, telling your kids and grandkids about the time. Author Jen Stanton writes, "Adventure leaves us with a new story to tell."

Adventure also offers opportunities for encounters with interesting and diverse people. Think about the people you have met on vacation, at campgrounds, during fishing and hunting trips, at that little coffee shop near Yellowstone. If you call yourself a Christian, these are not chance encounters, these are God arranged appointments designed to showcase Jesus to a dying world.

FINDING THE TRAIL

The Jesus Trail is one of the national treasures on Israel. Maon Inon, a Jewish entrepreneur who established hostels and guesthouses in Israel, and David Landis, a Christian hiking specialist, first developed the trail in 2007. Every year hundreds of people hike the trail. The usual starting point is Nazareth, the largest Arab town in Israel with a population of around 80,000. The trail ends at the Sea of Galilee.

We began planning and training for our adventure about six months in advance. Being the oldest member of the group, I began, what I considered, an aggressive regiment of hiking, running, and weight training.

Choosing my equipment was both fun and frustrating. Ultra-lightweight was the key consideration for me. The fewer pounds I had to carry the more likely I could keep up with the younger members of the group.

Researching the best tent, sleeping bag, hiking shoes, and other needed items became an obsession, I was determined to 'live up to my equipment." You can find a list of my equipment in Appendix-A in the back of this book.

Our team consisted on Dale Armstrong, Jim Zalenski, Mike Howell, Bill Huffman, and myself. Mike and Bill, two members of our party, had both been to Israel before and were avid students of biblical archeology. This, coupled with their military and law enforcement background, which included considerable time spent in the Middle East, added some unique perspectives to the trip. Be it navigation skills, common sense decision-making, or quiet strength, we all benefited from the pooled wisdom of the five.

In his excellent book, "Adventure is Everywhere," Matthew Walker says, "Adventures that have the greatest impact and leave the most indelible marks all share one common ingredient, that of great companionship."

I encourage you, when planning an adventure, and also during the adventure, to pray that God will give you insight into his divine character and take time to reflect on the blessings of life. When I'm away from distractions of work and family I treasure periods of solitude when I can focus on spiritual things and be more sensitive to God's voice.

During the Jesus Trail adventure I learned a lot about myself. I learned that I wasn't as fit as I thought I was. I learned that God blesses adventure. I learned that it's sometimes necessary to ask for help, and I learned an important lesson in perseverance.

The first day out on the trail we had covered about nine miles by lunchtime, a much faster pace that I was accustomed to. The first three miles were up the east side of Mount Tabor following steep streets. Most of our hiking on this day was on paved streets through small towns and villages, whereas my training had been on wooded dirt trails and roads, and the terrain here was much steeper here than I expected.

Passing through predominately Arab villages in the Jewish state of Israel was kind of unexpected. I guess I naively assumed that Arab Israeli's were more assimilated into the Jewish state, but like most modern democracy's many minorities still choose to live in enclaves. Bill and Mike told us you could normally distinguish the Arab homes by their flat roofs.

On the other side of Mount Tabor, we followed the Via Mares through the Plain of Megiddo. We saw the seven hills of Nazareth to the north. Approaching Nazareth I knew I was in trouble. Ahead lie a series of long and steep hills. My feet were already tenderized from blisters, while the heat of the day and the weight of my pack were beginning to also take their toll.

Leaving the blister-creating pavement, we were now on a dirt trail. I trudged slowly forward past olive groves and scrub oaks, lagging far behind the rest of the guys. Bill graciously stayed back with me as we could see Dale, Mike and Jim far ahead near the top of the last hill.

At about mid-point of the final accent, I hit a wall. I was dizzy and weak. Dale later said I looked as white as a sheet. I could go no further. I dropped my pack and sat down on an outcropping of rocks overlooking a small stream.

As I sat there trying to get my legs back under me, I thought of Jesus, who as a boy must have walked these same steep, dusty hills.

I took a drink from my second water bottle and ate half an energy bar. Dale and Jim came back to check on me. Dale grabbed my pack, tossed it on top of his fifty-pound backpack and without so much as a word, sprinted to the top of the hill.

Dale is a mountain of a man. He stands about six foot five inches tall and is strong as an ox. A kind, gentle soul, he loves the Lord and loves God's people. He's been a huge inspiration to me, and many others I know.

Emily Wing Smith once said, "Being soaked alone is cold. Being soaked with good friends is an adventure." That's the way I felt on that bright, clear morning on the trail near Nazareth.

With the encouragement of my fellow hikers I had persevered through a tough morning on the trail and after lunch I caught a ride to our campsite. After another seven-mile hike the other guys made it to where I was waiting at the camp. We chose a site in a beautiful stand of pines near the entrance of Zippori National Park.

Everyone was tired and hungry. The stars were bright and the night air was crisp and clear. During a relaxing time around a small campfire, Dale said, "God must love it when men get together around a campfire." Thoughts of the day linger as we turned in for the night.

Little did we know this was not going to be a restful night! The first hint of trouble came quickly. Two cars screeched in near the gate to the park and shut off their engines. The youthful occupants spilled out with loud talk, singing, and the incessant beat of what Jim later called "Arab-Techno" music. The party lasted until near dawn. Sometime during the night, a random person stumbled up the trail coming to near our camp. Seeing our tents, he quickly retreated to the party.

Israel is a tiny country about the size of the state of New Jersey surrounded by Arab states wishing to destroy them. The (IDF) Israel Defense Forces, and all who call Israel home, live with the constant threat of violence and must always remain vigilant.

Hearing the Muslim call to prayer from traditional Christian sites was somewhat unnerving. Several times during our trip we were reminded that Israel is a nation divided. Peaceful trails cross bitterly contested highways. Tranquil paths parallel barbed wire displaying signs warning of Land Mine Area, and smiling Christian tourists brush past stern Orthodox Jews and occasional hate-filled Muslims.

Over 1.4 million Arabs live in Israel today along with 6 million Jews. Most Arabs are peaceful citizens who can vote, serve in the Knesset, but cannot serve in the military. Some who live inside the country are radical and hate the Jews and Americans.

FOLLOWING THE TRAIL

Adventure offers experiences we can't find a home. Experiences, both good and bad, become the building blocks for a lifetime of stories. On day two we covered about thirteen miles. Up at 7:00 am, still groggy from little sleep, we explored the ancient ruins at Zippori, then continued northwest toward the village of Cana, where Jesus turned water into wine.

As we were coming up a steep hill, entering the village of Mash'had, (the traditional birthplace of the Prophet Jonah), a group of three or four Arab boys appeared from the front yard of a two-story home. I would guess them to be ten to twelve years of age. They began to hurl rocks and insults at us, and fire rubber pellets. I could see the sad anger and hate in their young faces. Mike was in the front of our group and as he would fake charge at them, they would retreat, and then quickly return for another round of rocks and rebellion. Thankfully no one was hurt.

We passed on as the adults of the home sat quietly on the second story porch seemingly unconcerned with what was happening in front of them. I'll have to give those four Arab kids credit, they were fearless, and had grit enough to challenge five adults, even if it was misguided, their perseverance and risk was purposeful.

I often think about those Arab kids and pray that they will find the peace that comes from knowing Jesus Christ and that someday they will learn to live at peace with their Jewish neighbors.

THE BENEFITS OF ADVENTURE

Adventure can involve risk. It's part of the experience men crave. Risk teaches us, helps form our character, and it's one of the benefits of adventure. Adventure is not productive in the normal sense of the word, but its benefits are plentiful.

Author Derek Loudermilk adds, "Other benefits of adventure include increased confidence, self-reliance, decision-making skills, a sense of freedom, learned survival skills, and joy. Whenever we complete a tough challenge it boosts our self-confidence and stretches us to adapt, to learn new ways, and to step out of the comfort zone of doing things the way we are accustomed to doing them."

Self-reliance is a skill lacking in many today. We expect others or the government to take care of us and many have lost the survival instincts our parents and grandparents had. Adventure offers many opportunities to improve decision-making skills. It might be something as simple as choosing the correct fork in the trail, determining the best location to build a campfire, or judging the distance to the next fresh water source.

I have noticed that many teens and millennial age young men appear overly cautious when it comes to attempting outdoor challenges. Perhaps it's their fear of failure, fear of the unknown, over protective parents, or their obvious lack of experience in the outdoors.

As the director of an outdoor adventure ministry called Rugged Faith, I see many young dads of boy's 10 to 15 years old who come to our Rugged Faith Boot Camps. These dads may have never shot a gun, ridden a 4-wheeler, caught a fish, hiked in the woods, shot a bow and arrow, or hunted a deer, and many don't own any outdoor gear.

To be fair, these are wonderful dads who love their kids and most are committed church members. They are good providers, they are involved in their community, and they have many life skills I, and other older men, may not possess.

My burden for these men is the fact they do not know what they are missing by never experiencing outdoor adventure. The inspiration gained from the sight of a brilliant sunrise over the mountains on a fall morning. The excitement of hooking a rainbow trout on a fly rod, or the heart-pounding sensation that comes when you spot a big buck coming toward your tree stand.

The Jesus Trail offers Christian men the opportunity to experience the Bible in a unique way. The stories you have read and the places you have heard about, come alive when you are actually there!

On the third day of hiking, we stopped for a rest on a level ridge-top overlooking the village of Cana and the valley to the north. Lunch consisted of a packet of tuna and some crackers, a Payday candy bar, and water. As I ate my meager lunch, I can't explain the peace that came over me. Just the fact I was in the Holy Land where Jesus lived was enough to inspire! Plus, the blessing of being with good friends, doing something I love, created a sense of satisfaction only children of God can know.

Throughout the afternoon, we hiked through open country following the paint- blazed trail markers. Up and down rugged hills, sometimes on pavement, mostly on dirt roads, past fields of what's called the Mediterranean Triad of olives, wheat, and grapes.

Whenever we passed a shop or country story we would stop and visit with the clerks or others customers or passersby and have mint lemonade, one of our favorite Jesus Trail treats.

That night we camped at Golani Junction, finding a wooded area just south of the main highway. It was littered with trash and was not an ideal campsite, but we were ready to get off our feet, so we made the best of it.

Night two on the trail was a more restful night without the techno music of the first night. We had dinner at a nearby McDonalds, returned to camp, built a big campfire and shared stories. We were up early and walked over to see a portion of ancient Roman Road once a major east-west thoroughfare. In this area, it runs through a field covered with huge prickly-pear cactus, you can still see deep ruts cut into the landscape.

It's reasonable to think Jesus and his disciples walked this very road on their way from Nazareth to the Sea of Galilee. The Apostle Paul most likely passed through here on his way to Damascus.

On Day three we took a break from the trail and caught a bus to the city of Tiberius on the banks of the Sea of Galilee. We rented a minivan and continued around the west side of what modern day Israelis call Lake Kinneret, a Hebrew word for harp.

This was the place! Around every corner the Bible was vividly displayed. You can just imagine fishing boats on the beach, villagers busy with daily chores and kids splashing in the azure blue water. I can almost hear Jesus telling Peter to "put out into deep water."

Chris Hutcheson writes the following, "The choice to live an adventurous lifestyle is not an easy one, it requires moxie. It is very difficult to break free of the monotonous routine of daily life when you have been repeating it for years on end." He goes on to say, "Perhaps it's time for men to seek to regain the element of adventure that originally drove those before us to cross oceans and vast expanses of unknown terrain with no hope of return. The trail requires perseverance, but the benefits are worth the effort."

"TRAIL THOUGHT #1"

What are some areas of your life where you have shown, or you need too show perseverance?

2

PARADISE OUTFITTERS...
SPIRITUAL DEVELOPMENT

THE OUTDOORS IS a tool God uses to draw men to himself. My life certainly has been changed by my time in the wilderness. I can recall many instances of seeking God while alone in the outdoors. A man's spiritual growth comes from spending time with God, be it in church, in a small group Bible study, or alone in God's great outdoor church. While time in the outdoors is certainly not a replacement for regular attendance in a strong, Bible teaching church, we can grow spiritually wherever we seek after God.

It's my prayer that the stories, and examples I gather on my adventures will offer proof of a Creator, and will inspire others to seek after God. Adventure offers opportunities for spiritual development, be it through fellowship with other believers, time spent in prayer, or trail time study from God's word.

In his Outdoor Leadership blog Ashley Denton says, "Over 100 times in the Bible the text explicitly identifies lives being changed because of a wilderness journey. Noah, Moses, Elijah, and Jesus all spent days in wilderness environments. Jesus shows us that the wilderness is a place where God gets our attention."

The mission of Rugged Faith Ministries is to offer men opportunities to experience God in the great outdoors. Our weekend retreats blend outdoor adventure activities and sound biblical teaching. We call it "Adventure with a Purpose;" that purpose being to call men to the saving knowledge of Jesus Christ.

FAITH FOR THE TRAIL

The shores of the Sea of Galilee showcase dozens of historic places. The first ones we encountered were the villages of Magadala, whose most famous resident was Mary Magdalene, and Tabgha, home of the Church of the Multiplication of Loaves and Fishes. It's almost sensory overload having so many famous sites in such a small area. While the biblical sites were interesting to visit, I preferred the open trail with fewer people.

With limited time to explore we moved on around the lake, we found a deserted stretch of shoreline and some of the guys took a swim in the cold, clear waters of the Sea of Galilee.

This area was not only home to four of the Disciples of Jesus: Peter, James, John, and Andrew, but Capernaum also served as the home base for Jesus' ministry in Galilee.

Standing next to a statue of Peter with the "keys to the kingdom" I imagined what he, and the Sons of Thunder; James and John, must have been like. I think of them as strong, aggressive men who gave up their lives to follow Jesus. I wonder what it was like for them growing up in this small fishing village?

We think of the disciples and other Bible characters as somehow being special, different from us. It's reassuring the God uses ordinary men to do extraordinary things. It's part of him outfitting us for service.

Think about men you admire, your hero's, aren't they usually men of action? Aren't they men of great courage, who have accomplished great things, and explored the outer limits of our planet?

I think about men of the Bible, giants of the faith, men like Moses, Caleb, Nehemiah, David, and the Apostle Paul. We can draw many valuable spiritual lessons from their lives and the adventures of these famous men. Again, the goal of adventure is to point others to Jesus Christ. In his book "How Women Help Men Find God" author David Murrow encourages us to "Think about how the great men of the Bible found their missions. Moses walked up the mountain. Jacob wrestled with God. David slew Goliath. Jesus plunged into the wilderness. A man's pursuit of God is often a physical experience as much as a mental one."

SEVEN IMPORTANT TRAITS OF ADVENTURE
In his book "The Explorers," Martin Dugard points out seven common traits all explorers possess. They include Perseverance, Curiosity, Hope, Passion, Courage, Independence and Self-Discipline.

Let's look at Dugard's seven common traits from the perspective of the adventurous Christian. The first is <u>Perseverance</u> a key trait of all successful explorers and adventurers.

Grit, moxie, stick-to-it, tenacity, resolute; these are just some of the synonyms of perseverance. I'm sure you have read many stories of tough-minded men who refuse to quit. I recently read one story that perfectly illustrates this important trait. Graham Hughes has visited all 201 countries in the world without flying any miles. His four-year adventure is called The Odyssey Expedition. Beginning January 1, 2009, Hughes set out to visit every nation on earth. People told him he was insane to try it, others said it was impossible, but he persevered. Travelling by boat, train, bus, car, on horseback, bicycle, and other ways he completed this amazing journey in 2013

James 1:12, provides us with an awesome promise concerning perseverance. James says, "Blessed is the one who perseveres under trial because, having stood the test, that person will receive the crown of life that the Lord has promised to those who love him."

Author Rick Johnson points out, "Unfortunately, quitting is an easily-learned habit of young males. We learn early in life to take the easiest route and avoid anything unpleasant. Boys who are rescued too often learn to quit. Then anytime something becomes difficult in life they quit or take pains to avoid it. They become conditioned and programmed to expect someone else (generally a woman) to come along and take care of it. These boys struggle throughout life and the people who depend on them suffer most."

The writer of Hebrews offers some sound advice on this subject. "Therefore, since we are surrounded by such a great cloud of witnesses, let us throw off everything that hinders, and the sin that so easily entangles, and let us run with perseverance the race marked out for us."

The second trait of all explorers is <u>Curiosity;</u> it pushes us to know more about creation and the Creator. We see God at every turn, the intricate leaves of an oak tree, the special design of the hummingbird, the majesty of a thunderstorm. Curiosity may have killed the cat, but it's a trait that drives men to seek after both adventure and God. Curiosity sparks the urge to seek. Blogger Martin Holland puts it this way. "I want to be an explorer; I have always wanted to be an explorer, because this restless state of curiosity and living at the edge is the best path to an exciting, challenging, fulfilling, and worthwhile life."

Are you curious about God? Do you seek to understand the mysteries of God? Curiosity is a key element in our spiritual growth. It creates a hunger to dig into scripture and to look forward to times of Bible study with other believers. Those who do not know God can't understand our fascination with the ancient book and its author.

<u>Hope</u> is the third trait, as Christians our hope is in Jesus Christ. It's not a worldly hope that maybe something good might happen. "I sure hope I get that job," or "I hope I go to heaven when I die." No, the hope we have is certain. Jesus has promised us eternal security if we will repent of our sins, turn from our sinful lifestyle, and accept Him as our personal savior. The emperor Napoleon once said, "A leader is a dealer in hope." For the Christian, God is our leader and he offers a winning hope the world cannot match.

<u>Passion</u> is the fourth trait of all explorers. Passion for life comes with knowing we have a purpose. Bill Hybels said, "God has equipped each one of us with a unique combination of personality, temperament and talents that he can use to impact this world for good." Passion follows purpose. When you know your purpose in life you can then live each day with passion. Is your passion the pleasures of this world or the things of God?

The fifth trait is <u>Courage,</u> sometimes defined as the absence of fear. The phrase "fear not" is recorded over 75 times in the Bible. I. Timothy 1:7 says, "For God has not given us a spirit of fear, but one of power, love, and sound judgment. "Courage is contagious." As men, we should cultivate courage in our sons, and in others by exposing them to regular times of adventure. In chapter 8 I'll talk more about contagious courage, cultivating courage, and the fact that courage flows from a concern over injustice

The sixth trait is <u>Independence</u>, which is closely related to self-reliance and is not a virtue extolled in Christianity. Rather, inter-dependence of bearing one another's burdens and being part of the family of God is commanded. Being somewhat of a loner, I struggle in this area. Many times, I prefer to go it alone, feeling I don't need anyone, but in my heart I believe Psalm 27:17, "As iron sharpens iron, so one man sharpens another."

The seventh and final trait all explorers possess is <u>Self-Discipline</u>. This important element of both adventure and faith is what allows us to grow. The Bible says to discipline yourself for the purpose of godliness; which is not possible without the Spirit of God living inside us. John MacArthur says, "Biblically, self-discipline may be summarized in one word: obedience. To exercise self-discipline is to avoid evil by staying within the bounds of God's law."

James 1:6-8 warns that the double-minded man is tossed about like a ship in a storm. When God say, "be transformed by the renewing of your minds," only then are we capable of self-discipline.

These seven common traits of the explorer can certainly apply to those who search for truth and find it in Jesus Christ. My friend Jim questioned, "How do we translate these physical adventures into the spiritual adventures the Lord really wants us to engage in? All seven traits are potential key elements in forging a Gospel pathway through our cultural wilderness."

From birth to death, Moses certainly had these traits in good measure. Men's Journal once said, "Moses was an adventurer from the start, as a baby he kayaked the Nile in a basket. Moses displayed perseverance during his forty-plus years in the wilderness. His curiosity drew him to the burning bush. His hope in God kept him pressing on. His passion was displayed when he killed an Egyptian. His courage was unmatched as he led 2 million people out of slavery. He grew in interdependence as he learned to delegate the workload. He showed self-discipline by shunning the perks of the palace and returning to his people.

Pastor Wes George points out that Moses finished strong. At his death, "his eyes were not weak his vitality had not left him." Nehemiah was another who processed these virtues. He was a wall builder whose example inspires us all to grow in faith.

As we grow in these seven important traits not only will our lives be better, but also others will notice our spiritual development and want to know our secret. Through His pruning of us, and His love for us, the God of paradise prepares us for the great adventure of the Christian life.

FRIENDS ON THE TRAIL

Finishing out our busy fourth day visiting several sites of biblical ruins including Bethsaida and Korazin, we enjoy an awesome dinner at St Peter's Fish house near En Gev, a small kibbutz situated at the foot of the Golan Heights.

We made camp on the beach on the east side of Sea of Galilee. While we set up our tents on the sand, one of the guys found a couple of old wooden pallets, and built a large campfire. A huge part of any adventure is the special times of conversation along the trail and around the campfire. Learning about the hopes, dreams, fears, and concerns of others and sharing life's joys and blessings with others build friendships to last a lifetime.

The sparks from the dry wood floated into the dusky sky, the opening act to an after dark show created by the city lights of Tiberius on the hills across the lake. The crisp nigh air amplified our conversations across the calm water.

During the days leading up to the trip there was a lot of discussion concerning the proper gear to carry. Weight is the enemy of the through hiker so my Big Agnes one-man tent worked perfectly on this trip. It's easy set up and lightweight 2.5 pounds make it the ideal backpackers choice.

For my sleeping gear, I chose the Marmot Hydrogen sleeping bag, and the Thermo-rest inflatable sleeping pad and pillow. A wise choice for a backpack is the Gregory Z-40, it's lightweight at 3.5 pounds yet roomy with lots of zippered compartments. On this chilly, blustery night, I was happy I followed the advice of friends who recommended this quality backpacking gear.

The next morning, we were up early. A blustery, overcast, and cold hike to visit the ruins at Hippos, tucked away on a steep hilltop above our campsite. Hippos is an archaeological site overlooking the Sea of Galilee. According to Josephus, a Jewish historian, Hippos was a pagan city, and a sworn enemy of the newer city of Tiberius across the lake. In the New Testament when Jesus mentions a "city set upon a hill cannot be hidden" He may have been referring to Hippos.

There are numerous historical sites in the area north of the lake. Banias and Tel Dan Waterfalls, which is one of the main tributaries forming the Jordan River, Caesarea Philippi with its Temple of Pan, and of course, the Mount of Beatitudes. Quoting from the Jesus Trail guidebook, "The Mount of Beatitudes is the traditional site of the Sermon on the Mount found in Matthew chapters 5-7. The word beatitudes means blessed."

The inspiration and historical Bible knowledge I gained on this trip has hopefully enhanced my effectiveness with Rugged Faith Ministries. Time spent in creation can bring us closer to the Creator. God equips us much the same way an outdoor outfitter equips an expedition.

Rugged Faith like so many other outdoor ministries strives to use the outdoors as a tool for helping men grow in their faith. Equipping men to lead others into the adventure that is the Christian life. Discipleship training is outfitting a man to carry the good news to those who are lost. I find that the school of the outdoors in a classroom where many men are more open to the gospel message than in a traditional church.

In the next few pages I want to highlight four outdoor ministries I think are doing an outstanding job of using the outdoors to reach men and youth for Christ. I have included a more complete list of outdoor ministries in Appendix-B in the back of this book. All these ministries are doing an awesome job, but regrettably I'm only able to feature these four.

Whether it's hunting, fishing, backpacking, kayaking, or camping, men are being creative in using God's great outdoors in way to minister to others.

In my digital search, I found dozens of ministries in every region of North America using the outdoors as a tool to reach men for Christ.

From fishing along the Florida Gulf Coast, to bear hunting in Canada; from ducking hunting in Delaware to sand dune buggy's in southern California, I found God's name being glorified through outdoor adventure ministry.

One of the most unique outdoor ministries is the *4th Musketeer USA,* located in Indianapolis, Indiana. The 4th Musketeers are an international ministry which began in Europe. Their web site says, "72 hours of inspiration, challenge and adventure. The 4th Musketeer (4M) is a men's movement that trains men to live for their King."

Their "Extreme Character Challenge" (XCC) is the heart of the ministry. The model of the XCC is cutting edge. "Character starts at the borders of the unknown." Men are pushed further, deeper, and harder than they may have ever experienced before. Fatigue, cold, hunger, thirst and physical exhaustion are emotions that men can expect.

My friend Jim Zalenski recently had the opportunity to participate in one of the Xtreme Character Challenges, he had this to say, "Having just completed the Arkansas Xtreme Character Challenge I encourage you to commit a week-end to this life-changing experience. It as one of the most difficult things I've ever done and certainly one of the most rewarding."

Another outdoor ministry I have come to respect is based in Tulsa, Oklahoma. *Cave Time Ministries* and its founder Jeff Voth have become good friends and have "Locked Shields' as Jeff likes to say, with our ministry, Rugged Faith.

Voth says, "Cave Time offers men a refuge, a place of safety, a place to escape. When David was under assault and mere steps ahead of death, he escaped to a place that was familiar to him–The Cave, a place of refuge.

Overcome by the assaults of debt, distress, and discontentment, the greatest warriors of the day were also searching for a refuge–a place where they could find their strength, honor, and bare their souls without judgment. They found refuge and safety in the cave. Something happened in the cave, because they were referred to as Mighty Men."

Every year in September, Cave Time hosts its national conference they call "Cave Time USA." Hundreds of men and women from all over the nation attend this 3-day event.

Jeff goes on to say, "Cave Time is a call. It's a call to you and to every man. It's a call to show up and learn how to live like what you were created to be...a real man. Real men show up. Real men have Cave Time."

Solid Rock Outdoor Ministries (SROM) in Laramie, Wyoming offers what they call "Transformational Wilderness Expeditions." Executive Director, Andrew Arnold says," SROM is a premier Christ-centered deep wilderness ministry. SROM's mission is to birth and grow mature Christ followers who make disciples of all nations.

At SROM, the wilderness is a context for discipling Christians to be influential leaders in their communities and circles of influence. Their programming activities include backpacking, rock climbing, mountaineering, backcountry cooking, alpine and backcountry living, and authentic community building.

The final outdoor ministry to be highlighted is Spiritual Outdoor Adventures located in Nashville, Tennessee. Jimmy Sites founded SOA in 2002 as a local TV show. Today SOA has grown to become one of the highest-rated and most watched outdoor shows among all the hunting channels. Jimmy has also created the "Heart of the Outdoors" Bible for sportsmen. Over $1.3 million worth of these Bible have been distributed since it was produced. SOA distributes the Bibles at "Faith Nights' at professional baseball parks and at wild game dinner event where Sites speaks. Dr. Sites travels the world filming hunting the fishing expeditions and always includes the gospel message into all his programs.

These four outdoor ministries are making a difference in the lives of men. Equipping men, leading in discipleship training by introducing men to the joys of creation and the love of the Creator. For more information about these and many other outdoor ministries take look at Appendix-B in the back of this book.

"TRAIL THOUGHT #2"

How do we translate physical adventures into the spiritual adventures God really wants us to be engaged in?

3

BOOT CAMP ...CREATING MEMORIES

MEMORIES ARE MADE during times of adventure. Those memories are the elements of a full life. They are always with us. Even now, almost six years later, I still recall the adventure we had along the Jesus Trail.

Blogger Candice Andrews recently wrote, "Going on adventures fosters reflectiveness, a mental skill often in short supply today. Adventures give us pleasant memories, which we often bring back to the forefront of our minds for reminiscing. This means that our journeys marinate a while, an especially valuable exercise these days when we're all so perpetually busy that most of what we do passes by in a flash and is gone forever — without having any real meaning attached to it. But reliving our adventures again and again allows us the time — and capability — to learn something from them."

Memories of places, experiences, and the people we meet pays dividends for years to come. Some of my fondest memories are of times spent in the outdoors. Meaningful experiences of family camping trips, winter days spent at deer hunting camps with great storytellers, and encounters with interesting people I met during outdoor adventures.

Derek Loudermilk of the Good Men Project says, "One measure of a man is his impact on the people around him. Adventures provide stories, examples and proof for others to learn from."

We met some interesting people during our time in Israel. Most were warm and helpful. I recall an encounter at the train station in Tel Aviv. The parking lot outside the terminal was abuzz with youthful looking soldiers returning from weekend passes, thus, we were not having much success catching a bus to Mount Tabor. A voice from a row of taxies and mini-buses got our attention, "You need ride? You need taxi to Kavor Tavor (Mount Tabor)?"

We asked about the cost, the driver gave us what seemed like a reasonable amount. We looked at each other in agreement, and hopped inside a less than stellar looking minivan.

Our two, yes two, guides were very talkative! We learned the one riding shotgun was Isak Yarimi. Seven years ago, he had moved to Israel from Poland, and like us, was hitching a ride north to his home near Elit.

About ten minutes into our ride the van coughed, quivered and then completely died, right in the middle of a busy four-lane highway. The driver hastily jerked the still gliding hunk over to the right-hand lane. So, what do we do now? The driver called somebody. It seemed that no help was expected for several hours. "Will it start if we push it?" Maybe. We piled out of the side door, dodging oncoming traffic and began pushing the van down the busy expressway. The driver popped the clutch; the beast roared to life, we were back in business.

These two individuals we met were a part of the backpack full of memories from this awesome adventure.

PEOPLE, PROCESS, AND PRODUCT

People, process, and product form the progressive business philosophy of the TV show "The Prophet" with Marcus Lemonis who helps businesses that are struggling by resolving conflicts between owners, fine-tuning the flow of the business and fixing financial or design issue with the products.

People, process, and product should also be our order of emphasis in ministry. *People* always come first. It's all about the people. The *process* is all about our ongoing sanctification as we become more like our heavenly Father. The *product* is the program or projects we offer to strengthen God's kingdom. Process and product must always follow our love and concern for others.

Are you more concerned about the details, process, and routine of life while forgetting that the Christian life is all about the people? 1 Corinthians 13:1 says, "If I speak human or angelic languages but do not have love, I am a sounding gong or a clanging cymbal."

Rugged Faith Boot Camp is all about people. We strive to create outdoor adventure opportunities for men, which are both exciting and memorable. A question we asked early and often as we developed the various aspects of the Boot Camp was, "Will it be memorable?"

We offer opportunities for wonderful, relaxing Christian fellowship, as well as biblical based messages that help equip and grow men in their faith. As we grow in our love for God, we supernaturally grow in our love for other people. Men who attend out camps tell us they love the outdoor activities and the great food, but what they remember most is the people. Those special times around the campfire, or those one-on-one conversations while fishing or sharing a cup of coffee with a buddy makes boot camp memorable.

Studies by neurologist David Eangleman show, "The more detailed the memory, the longer the moment seems to last. The more familiar the world becomes, the less information your brain writes down, and the more quickly time seems to pass."

I'm not sure I completely buy this study, but I do know that lasting memories created during times of adventure are a well of inspiration to draw from. The times I remember most are those that involved adventure, other people, and a tough challenge I completed.

Jon Krakauer, in his bestselling book, "Into the Wild", points out, "The very basic core of a man's living spirit is his passion for adventure. The joy of life comes from our encounters with new experiences, and hence there is no greater joy than to have an endlessly-changing horizon, for each day to have a new and different sun."

Most of the men who attend our boot camps come with a group of men from a church. We have found that men enjoy the experience more when they are with friends and relatives.

The boot camp offers unique opportunities for outreach to unbelievers in their community. Many times, we meet un-churched men who attend, primarily for the fellowship and the activities, and leave knowing Jesus, or being drawn one step closer to Him, because of these Spirit-filled times in the outdoors.

BIBLE LAND MEMORIES
The Jesus Trail adventure included visits to many ancient Tels or villages. Mike and Bill shared several fascinating biblical archeology

lessons at places like Hazor, Tel Dan and Megiddo. I will always remember those special days walking where Jesus walked.

Five days into the trip, the Hooha Hostel near Mount Tabor became our home away from home. On another night we camped at Mount Carmel, site of Elijah's throw-down with the 450 prophets of Baal. We found no vacancy at the local campgrounds, so we pulled off on a dirt road, drove a mile of so, and made camp under some scrubby trees in the edge of a dusty cow pasture. We felt safe doing this in Israel and camping out aligned our hearts closely with Jesus; as if we were truly seeing through his eyes.

In I Kings 18 we find one of my favorite stories in all of Scripture, the story of an ultimate outdoor challenge on Mount Carmel. In ancient culture, high places were frequently considered to be sacred, and Mount Carmel appears to have been no exception.

Elijah challenged 450 prophets of Baal to a contest at the altar on Mount Carmel to determine whose god was really in control of the Kingdom of Israel. It was a showdown at God's OK Corral. After the prophets of Baal had prayed, pleaded, and failed, Elijah poured water on his sacrifice to saturate the altar and then as he prayed, fire fell and consumed the sacrifice, wood, stones, soil and water. The Israelite witnesses proclaimed, "The LORD, He is God! The LORD, He is God!"

Elijah said to Ahab, "Go get something to eat and drink, for I hear a mighty rainstorm coming!" So, Ahab went to eat and drink. Meanwhile, Elijah climbed to the top of Mount Carmel and bowed low to the ground and prayed with his face between his knees.

He then said to his servant "Go and look out toward the sea." The servant went and looked, then returned to Elijah and said, "I didn't see anything." Seven times Elijah told him to go and look. Finally, the seventh time, his servant told him, "I saw a little cloud about the size of a man's hand rising from the sea."

Elijah shouted, "Hurry to Ahab and tell him, 'Climb into your chariot and go back home. If you don't hurry, the rain will stop you," and soon the sky was black with clouds. A heavy wind brought a terrific rainstorm, and Ahab left quickly for Jezreel."

Beginning with a little cloud about the size of a man's hand, God brought rain to end the long drought. What an amazing example of God's faithfulness and his almighty power.

LIVING WATER

If you have ever been in a desert without water, you can appreciate this story! Much of Israel is a desert and several times on our Jesus Trail hike we were made aware of the importance of water to this region.

Near Zippori, and again at Megiddo, we explored huge systems of water storage tunnels and pits. A well has been discovered in the Kidron Valley south of Jerusalem, dug to a depth of 125 feet through solid limestone.

The city of Caesarea was supplied with water by means of two aqueducts, one taking water from springs on the southern slope of Mount Carmel, eight miles north, and the other bringing water from the Crocodile River, six miles north.

The temple at Jerusalem was supplied with water not only from large underground cisterns but also from an aqueduct that brought water from the Hebron hills. This aqueduct is forty-two miles long, and precisely graded to ensure a gentle flow of water, winding its way round hills.

REMEMBER PARTNERS IN MINISTRY

Water has been a key element in the success of our ministry, lasting memories flow out of our times along beautiful Ozark streams.

Rugged Faith Ministries has been blessed to partner with some amazing people who have allowed us to host our Rugged Faith Boot Camps at their facilities. These amazing upstream adventures have been the source of countless lives transformed whenever God's word is poured out.

We began these ministry adventures at Shepherd of the Ozarks, located deep in the Ozark Mountains, near Marshall, Arkansas. SOTO, as they have come to be known, is a fantastic facility located on Big Creek, near the Buffalo River National Park.

Big Creek twists southeastwardly and merges with The Buffalo River. The Buffalo River flows for about 150 miles through northwest Arkansas and is a national treasure. It's one of the few remaining free-flowing rivers in the nation, and in 1972 was the first National River to be designated in the United States.

Norfolk River Resort, near Mountain Home, Arkansas was kind enough to work with us in the early stages of the ministry. This facility is one of the premier trout fishing resorts in the south. With boat rentals, large cabins, and a conference center, Norfork River Resort has a truly spectacular location at the confluence of the Norfork and the White Rivers in northwest Arkansas. I grew up on the White River and know it well. I remember my brothers and I spending countless summer days along the banks of this clear, cold stream. Hunting, fishing, and camping are memory factories for kids of all ages.

Another group that has partnered with our ministry is Spring Valley Ranch, located on the banks of Spavinaw Creek, near Jay, Oklahoma. Sam and Stacy Jones, the owners of Spring Valley Ranch, have played an important roll in the growth of Rugged Faith Ministries. The Jones have become close friends and mentors who share our vision of using outdoor adventure to reach and equip men for Christian living.

Spring Valley Ranch, and the Jones other ranch, <u>The Flying J Bird Ranch,</u> are both first class facilities offering lodging, bird hunting, sporting clays, horseback riding, ATV tours, and fishing.

<u>Rockford Grange at Bear Hollow Ranch</u> is an amazing place. With over 1,500 acres of hills and valleys on the banks of Big Sugar Creek, this facility is a dream-come-true for outdoorsmen. With miles of ATV trails, first class archery and handgun shooting ranges, and great fishing, this place is a gift from God.

These four facilities, all located on the banks of clear mountain streams, have allowed Rugged Faith Ministries to offer events that speak to the hearts of men. Our partnership with these groups has served as a reservoir that God has drawn from to transform lives, restore broken relationship, and create lasting memories.

MEMORIES OF LIVING WATER

Water also played an important role in Jesus' ministry. I mentioned his first miracle at Cana where he turned water into wine. The Bible mentions many other times water played an important role in the life and ministry of Jesus. In John 7:37-39, Jesus is known as the source of "Living Water." He tells the people, "If anyone is thirsty, let him come unto me and drink. He who believes in Me, from his innermost being will flow rivers of living water."

In John 4 we find the story of the woman at the well. Jesus tells her, "If you knew the gift of God and who it is that asks you for a drink, you would have asked him and He would have given you living water."

The imagery of living water is powerfully illustrated at one of my favorite places we visited on our trip to Israel. En Gedi is a large oasis with springs, waterfalls, and pools. It's located in the hills along the western shore of the Dead Sea, almost 1,200 feet below sea level.

With palm and willow trees, En Gedi is one of the few fresh water springs in this part of Israel.

We parked our minivan at the visitor center just off the main highway, leaving our backpacks in the car, then making our way up a steep, dusty trail toward the springs. I was surprised to see wild Ibex goats roaming freely around us. In Hebrew, En Gedi means "spring of the goat."

The Bible records that about 3,000 years ago, David hid from King Saul in the many caves around En Gedi. What a thrill for me to scramble up the same rocks and caves David did, before taking a dip under "David's Waterfall."

Looking back down the valley we saw the Dead Sea and the Mountains of Moab. Here I saw the stark contrast between the living water of En Gedi and dead water in the salty Dead Sea. This land gives us a picture of how God gives eternal life to those who accept him, but death brings eternity in hell for those who reject him.

OUTDOOR ADVENTURE MEMORIES

Wilderness settings, mountain solitude, and the beauty of nature, offer men time alone with God which most can't find in their everyday, fast-paced world. Someone once said, "Maybe the best way to recharge is to unplug from our high-tech world and get back to nature."

Ashley Denton of Outdoor Leadership says, "most adventure is about getting out of your comfort zone to open yourself up to the experiences and beauty that God gives you." Do you want to experience more of God? Do you want to grow in your relationship with the one who is the source of living water? Then go outside. Take a hike. Determine today that you will take time for adventure.

Rich Wagner asks, "The question most Christian men wrestle with is how to pursue a life of adventure when he is married, raising kids, and paying a mortgage?" Wagner's book is entitled "The Expeditionary Man." This thoughtful work has helped me answer this tough question and hopefully will help you balance your pursuits with your responsibilities.

Pastor Doug Self of The Orchard a church, located in Carbondale, Colorado, says, "Adventure is not always about going away to some exotic destination, but about finding excitement in both the new and the old."

Self offers the men of his church a unique opportunity to experience the outdoors. Each year Self guides a group of his men to the mountains for a weekend he calls "Bullets and Bibles." The men study God's Word, fellowship; hike the mountains, and enjoying target-shooting competition. Men look forward to this annual trip and many take their sons along for lasting memories.

Self reminds us, "Adventure can be found in our every day lives, in the little things. Adventure is about seizing opportunities and taking on life with passion, enthusiasm and excitement."

Outdoor Adventure Ministry (OAM) is gaining in popularity across the nation because it provides exciting outreach opportunities for men of a local church.

Self says, "We are seeing God's kingdom advance as men encounter Christ, through adventure."

"TRAIL THOUGHT #3"

Describe a meaningful memory from a time you spent in the outdoors, or on an adventure.

4

THE OUTDOOR CHURCH...IMPACT

I N AN ATTEMPT to make little or no lasting impact on the wilderness, the backpacker ethic tells us to "Take only pictures, and leave only footprints." Sadly, today many have adopted this as the theme for their Christian life and leave little or no trace of Jesus.

Some of the most impactful stories in the bible revolve around David. More has been written about David than any other Bible character other than Jesus. In this chapter, we want to look at how adventure can equip you to impact those around you.

On day 6 of the trip we drove about forty-five minutes southwest of Jerusalem to the Valley of Elah. This is the traditional site of the epic battle between David and Goliath. Flanked by the gently rolling hills of Judea, today this area is home to Israel's wine country.

We pulled over to the wide shoulder of the highway and scrambled down the steep road bank to a dry creek bed. Bible lore says this is the area where David picked up five stones for his battle with Goliath.

Secular history and I Samuel 17 in the Bible tell us the battle happened about 1010 BC, after the Philistines attempted to push along the Valley of Elah towards the heart of the kingdom of Judah. King Saul and his Israelite army blocked them, facing the Philistines at Sochoh in the center of the valley.

The Philistine giant, Goliath, of the nearby city of Gath, challenged the Israelites to fight him to determine the fate of the battle. No Israelite soldier dared to take this challenge, only young David, an untrained shepherd who came to assist his elder brothers, bravely volunteered for this fight. The two camps watched the fight from both sides of the valley.

God had rejected King Saul, and as a result, he was paralyzed with fear. The Army of the Living God has been sitting petrified without a willing leader. Fear is an impact killer. Fear is the opposite of courage, which is required to make an impact. You know the story and when David was victorious, the Israelite army was super-charged by his courageous actions. Courage is contagious!

I walked slowly down the dried-up creek, trying to picture the battle forces on the nearby hills. I could almost hear the taunts from the one side and the cheers from the other. I reached down and pick up five smooth stones and placed them in the pocket of my North Face windbreaker; souvenirs of a place I will never forget.

The exploits like of David and his mighty men and the impact they had on the nation of Israel have inspired me to search out new adventures, and to ask God to renew my courage so that I may impact a dying world. In Chapter nine we will dig deeper into the adventures of David. I encourage you to re-read this exciting story of the battle that made David a national hero and saved a nation, or go online and walk through the valley using Google maps.

THE CHURCH NEEDS IMPACT MEN

Today we need the men of the church of America to face the giants who are attacking our culture. Secular Humanism, apathy, materialism, false doctrine, and pornography are all destructive giants that must be slayed.

In his book, "Esau Rising; Ancient Adversaries and the War for America's Soul," author Bill Cloud makes the point that those who believe in God and the Bible are under attack. The author says, "Esau and his brother Jacob represent two different attitudes people have toward life. What Esau represents is that mindset, that lifestyle that would be willing to give away things that are sacred, in this case the birthright. Things that are holy. Things that are of eternal value. And he does it for something that is as common as a bowl of soup. What we try to do is establish the fact that what happened long ago is a pattern for what's happening right now."

In the Old Testament we learn that Easu and his decedents were rebellious people. They were anti-God of the Bible. Just as in the time of David, this "Spirit of Easu" is alive across the world, seeking to destroy Christians and annihilate the nation of Israel.

The church needs strong men. Men need the church to make an impact. Men need to hear the bold message that Jesus Saves! The church needs men with vitality and over-the-top enthusiasm for Jesus.

The idea for this kind of unique church, a special place designed with the sportsman in mind, had been bouncing around in my head for several years, a place with masculine music that men could relate too, and sermons offering a blend of adventure stories and sound biblical teaching.

Two years ago, we saw our dream of a church for sportsmen come true. With valuable input of my friends Brian Center, Jim Zalenski, and many others, along with a vital partnership with First Baptist Church of Rogers, Arkansas, <u>Rugged Faith Sportsman's Fellowship</u> became a reality.

Starting a new church is an adventure, and planting a new church is never easy. We have had many struggles and some doubts we were going to survive. Many men feel they don't need to attend church that they can experience God in the outdoors while hunting or fishing. They can to a limited degree, but to mature in their faith, men need to be part of a Bible believing fellowship of like-minded people. Men need men. As Proverbs 27:17 says, "As Iron sharpens iron, so one man sharpens another."

The odds are against any new church plant being successful. Ed Stetzer of Lifeway Research says about 80 percent of new church plants fail in the first three years. Impact requires time, and many churches quit too soon.

Stetzer goes on to say, "Church planting is not easy. And not all plants succeed. Some thrive, some grow slowly, some plateau early, and some jus' don't work. The reasons are different for every situation, but in every instance, there are lessons to be learned."

Reasons for failure include the wrong leadership, wrong location, lack of financial support, disunity among the core group, and the wrong church fit for the community.

The founders of Rugged Faith Sportsman's Fellowship wanted to focus on the men. We have always believed that to impact the lives of families we must first reach the men. Many men who love the outdoors do not attend a traditional church service on Sunday because they are in the woods hunting, on the lake fishing, or involved in other outdoor activities. With this in mind, we meet on Thursday evenings.

Author David Murrow reminds us "Young churches are magnets to men, because they are built on values men find attractive. Values like goal oriented, outwardly focused, and they require strategic planning and bold initiatives."

The term sportsman encompasses a broad range of interest depending on your region of the country. On the west coast, it may be surfing and rock climbing. In the Ozarks, where we are located, hunters and fishermen are the two major groups we have focused to reach.

We felt that if we focused on the hardcore hunter and fisherman, we would naturally attract other sportsmen whose main interest might be camping, backpacking, mountain biking, and others who love the outdoors. In our area, we are blessed to have an abundance of great fishing, whitetail deer hunting, as well as black bear, and small game like squirrel and rabbit.

THE IMPACT TEAM

The Rugged Faith Sportsman's Fellowship church plant has been a team effort. We had a core leadership group and leadership from a great church. Valuable input from Tim Wicker and others at the Arkansas Baptist State Convention has been God-given. I love a challenge and sadly I usually like to go alone, but as Leon McCarron says, "There's a lot to be said for facing challenges alone, for only then do we truly know what we are capable of, but to share joys, fears, and surprises is remarkably special."

Church is not a building; it's a group of people sharing life together as they grow in their faith and share the good news of Jesus Christ. God says, "I will build my church, but without the support of a dedicated group of volunteers as well as the guidance of an established church, a new church dramatically reduces it chances to survive.

Much discussion and prayer preceded our church launch. We spent hours developing a vision and mission statement. What day and time will we meet? Who will be the primary Bible teacher? What should the format look like, how can we best impact our community, how will we handle child-care, and many other concerns?

Rugged Faith Sportsman's Fellowship is a campus of First Baptist Church in Rogers, Arkansas. FBC Rogers is blessed to have many talented sportsmen as part of the leadership team.

Senior Pastor Wes George of FBC Rogers, an avid hunter, sets the vision and leads the team. Without the extraordinary biblical leadership of Pastor George, and the generous financial support of FBC Rogers, Rugged Faith Sportsman's Fellowship could not exist.

Jim Shaw, Discipleship Pastor and the Teaching Pastor at Rugged Faith, directs the day-to-day operations of the Rugged Faith campus. Pastor Shaw is a team builder who loves the outdoors, especially when it comes to hunting turkey, duck and deer.

THE ANTI-IMPACT MAN

In his book "Jesus Never Told us to Plant Churches" Pastor Trinity Jordan_warns us of those who will try to hijack a new church plant. Below he gives a brief description of each of these potential hijackers who seek to limit or destroy the impact of a new church plant.

"The Fixer, they feel God has called them to come fix you or the new church. Mr. Tunnel Vision, who wants the church to focus on one thing. Mr. Romantic, who fantasizes about what a perfect church should look like. Mr. Negative, nothing is ever right, they are toxic, get rid of them. Mr. Anti-Church, who feels that the modern-day church is wrong. Mr. Jack Russell Terrier, who can't settle on one thing, can't stay focused and drives everybody crazy. Mr. Supporter, whose vision just doesn't fit with what we are doing,"

Jordan's book warns church planters of those who seek to disrupt and destroy their efforts. To avoid these pitfalls, we spent time in prayer and in researching what others had done. It's best to learn from the mistakes of others than to learn from your own mistakes.

COPY WINNERS FOR IMPACT

Churches that target cowboys and bikers have been around for several years, but the sportsman's church is a relatively new concept.

The first church for sportsmen I can find any record of opened in 2004 in Missoula, Montana. The Outdoorsmen's Church, founded by Mark Hasenyager, their slogan is, "Outfitting the Body to Rescue the Searching." Today the Outdoorsmen's Church has grown to three campuses in the state of Montana.

Before we launched our sportsman's church we spoke with several men who have blazed the trail of sportsman's church including Brodie Swisher, Sportsman's Church in Paris, TN, Glen Dry of the Sportsmen's Church, in Victoria, TX, Pastor Brandon Smith founder of Paradise Outfitters near Kansas City, Missouri, Mark Hasenyager of Outdoorsmen's Church in Missoula, Montana, and Scottie Johnson, founder of The Outdoor Church of Arkansas located in Conway, Arkansas.

These men shared valuable lessons and advice, which prevented us from making many early mistakes as well as saving us valuable time and money.

CHURCH ON THE MOVE

On the afternoon of day 6 we drive south from the Valley of Elah we enter the Negev, a desolate desert area stretching from Beersheba in the north to the city of Eilat on the Gulf of Aqaba. The Negev makes up over half of the nation of Israel. With its rocky, dusty, multi-shades of brown and its many box canyons, deep craters, and wadis, the Negev is sparsely populated with a few hardy villagers and nomadic Bedouins.

We rode in silence as the stark beauty of the area leaves one speechless. It's a lonely, yet peaceful place like none I have experienced. It can be a worship experience in itself to travel the Holy Land. Reminders of biblical characters and Bible stories are around every corner. The sights, sounds, and smells all blend to form a special memory.

As we drove deeper into Negev on the mostly deserted two-lane highway, I thought about the ancient warring tribes of Canaanites, Amalekites, and Edomites who once roamed this parched land. Worshipping pagan gods like Baal, Asherah, and Pam; these groups waged an intense battle for the hearts and minds of God's people.

Step, step, step, one foot in front of the other, walking gives one focus. No more busy traffic, cell phones, time away from the constant noise of TV and the pull of the computer. Walking the trail gives you time to meditate on the big questions of life. Deep question of purpose, legacy, and impact fill each step. I'm reminded that I am a part of His church on the move, how can I better serve my fellowman.

Be it Abraham, Moses, John the Baptist, or today's leaders, God calls men to the wilderness adventure so they can be refreshed, and then sent back into battle to influence their world for good.

Author Peter Ives says, "We may view the Old Testament desert fathers as crazy for retreating into the wilderness, but maybe they did this because they valued being pure more than being useful. Can we at least appreciate that these desert hermits were more interested in who they were becoming rather than being preoccupied with what they were producing."

TRAILBLAZERS

Sportsman's church planters are trailblazers. They boldly strike out into new areas battling discouragement, expecting little earthly reward, and always with the risk of complete failure. These adventure-minded leaders follow God's call to take the gospel to a group of un-churched people with no clear road map other then the Bible, prayer, and the call to make a difference.

Paradise Outfitters perfectly describes the goal of the sportsman's church. Equipping men and women for the Christian life. Giving them the tools, the gear, and the knowledge to be committed followers of Jesus Christ.

Much like a wilderness outfitter, who provides the necessary gear and guidance for a successful elk hunt, these pastors of sportsman's churches blaze the trail so men can experience the great adventure of following the Creator.

Pastor Brandon Smith is one such leader. About six years ago, Smith began a small group Bible study in his home. Through many challenges, moving two steps forward, then one-step back, slowly and faithfully the church began to grow.

Using their indoor archery leagues, car shows, church-wide camping trips, and other creative ministries, Paradise Outfitters has seen God grow the church to over three hundred people.

The outdoors is a powerful tool for reaching men for Christ. The American Wildlife Federation survey reports that over 14 million people in America describe themselves as hunters, and over 11 million describe themselves as sport fishermen.

P. J. Weeks of Rain Down Ministries says," When God created man he didn't place him in a nice air-conditioned office building. He placed him in the outdoors. Ever since creation men feel most alive in the great outdoors."

Weeks goes on to say," The trail and the woods are great equalizers. There is no special status among sportsmen. Except for the cost of their equipment and clothing, the wealthy businessman or doctor and the unemployed janitor are the same in a tree stand or duck blind. Both have the same goals, both the same sense of excitement, and equal opportunity for success."

In his book, "Hiking Through," Paul Stutzman points out, "The outdoors is a common denominator, and it bridges the gap between creation and the creator. The outdoors is an outlet for building friendships. Brotherhood, like that of David and Jonathan can be formed in the outdoors."

IMPACTFUL DISCOVERY

Day seven was another exciting day of discovery in the Holy Land. Hiking through the Negev was a special adventure. In the area around Qumran we left the visitors center and hiked up a narrow canyon. Ascending slowly along the rugged hillside, we laughed and joked, as men will do, a band of brothers, sharing life's unique experiences. I was thankful for the challenge this land offers.

Pastor and avid outdoorsman Zeke Pipher says, "Men who don't have healthy ways to experience risk and challenges tend to find harmful ways. Many men shrivel up inside when they're not regularly involved in some form of adventure." Serious problems follow bored men."

Located about one mile from the northwest shore of the Dead Sea, in the caves of Qumran, is where the now famous Dead Sea Scrolls were found in 1947. The following is how Will Varner of Associates for Biblical Research describes the discovery.

"Juma was beginning to get nervous. Some of his goats were climbing too high up the cliffs. He decided to climb the face of the cliff himself to bring them back. Little did Juma realize as he began his climb on that January day in 1947 that those straying goats would eventually involve him in "the greatest archaeological discovery in the twentieth century."

Such thoughts were far from his mind when he saw two small openings to one of the thousands of caves that dot those barren cliffs overlooking the northwestern shore of the Dead Sea. He threw a rock into one of the openings. The unexpected cracking sound surprised him; what else could be in those remote caves but treasure? He called to his cousins, Khalil and Muhammed, who climbed up and heard the exciting tale.

The youngest of the three, Muhammed, rose the next day before his two fellow "treasure-seekers" and made his way to the cave. The cave floor was covered with debris, including broken pottery. Along the wall stood several narrow jars, some with their bowl-shaped covers still in place.

Frantically, Muhammed began to explore the inside of each jar, but no treasure of gold was to be found… only a few bundles wrapped in cloth and greenish with age. Returning to his cousins, he related the sad news—no treasure. No treasure indeed! The scrolls those Bedouin boys removed from that dark cave that day, and the days following, would come to be recognized as the greatest manuscript treasure ever found—the first seven manuscripts of the Dead Sea Scrolls!"

Today many of the Dead Sea Scrolls can be seen in Jerusalem at the Shrine of the Book Museum and will soon be on display at the new Museum of the Bible in Washington, DC

The Bible is an adventure itself. It's God's instructions given to us for godly living. A church is just a building if it is not built on God's Word. Biblical teaching stressing the message of the gospel leads to transformed lives.

CREATIVE MINISTRY IMPACTS
The indoor archery range, the weekly meal, personal testimonies, and weekly Sportsman's Seminars are all designed to draw sportsmen to

Rugged Faith Sportsman's Fellowship. These fun activities are all a part of the process of reaching our community for Christ. The real heart of the church is Jesus. The fun stuff is only the appetizer, the main course is the story of God's love found in the Bible. One very well received segment of our church fellowship is the weekly Sportsman's Seminar. Every week we invite some local and regional outdoor sports personalities to come and share their expertise.

Seminar presenters include turkey callers; fly fisherman, dog trainers, mountain bikers, deer hunters, camping guys, MMA enthusiasts, college football coaches, and many others. I have enclosed a complete list of our seminar presenters in Appendix-D in the back of this book.

If you are looking for an adventure, you don't have to go to Israel, look no further that the new church plants in your community. Join in, and get involved. You don't have to leave your local church to be involved, who says you can't serve at two churches?

As I write this, Rugged Faith Sportsman's Fellowship is eighteen months old. It's a baby church with a lot of growing to do. But, with God's grace and a committed core, we believe this sportsman's church is on the upward path to becoming a healthy and vibrant church.

"TRAIL THOUGHT #4"

Consider ways you can make a godly impact on your family, in your church, your workplace, your community, and your nation. List some here.

5

FINDING PURE ADVENTURE ...PASSION

SEVEN DAYS INTO the trip, we turned our rental van left at Tel Arad, in the middle of nowhere, then drove another fifteen miles on a crooked, desolate highway to arrive at the backside of the mountain fortress of Masada. Masada is one of the most fascinating places I have ever been. Located on the southern edge of the Judean Wilderness, this ancient fortress is one of the most popular tourist attractions in all of

Israel. Herod the Great build this amazing complex around the year 35 BC. Situated on top of an isolated mesa, Masada overlooks the Dead Sea to the east.

Mike pulled the minivan up to the park entrance. The attendant informed us the campground was closed for the day. No worries, we parked the car, grabbed water bottles and cameras before beginning the trek up the eastside of the 1,300-foot mountain. It was getting late in the day, so we had the trail all to ourselves.

To the left of a well developed walking path we saw where the siege ramp was constructed by the Roman army around the years 73-74 AD. The trail was steep with several switchbacks but had handrails and man-made stairs in some places. The setting sun was still intense but the powdery dust underfoot made for easy walking.

At the top, the views were incredible and the ancient ruins well -preserved. The harsh climate and remoteness of Masada have protected the structures from destruction by man.

The passionate stand of the 960 Jewish zealots who died here in 73 AD has become an inspiration to the small nation of Israel. The zealots occupied the fortress during the Revolt of the Jews against Roman rule.

The Roman Tenth Legion marched against the fortress determined to end the Jewish rebellion. For three years, the zealots were able to hold out against the ten thousand Roman soldiers encamped at the base of the mountain. Finally, the Romans build a massive siege ramp up the eastside and pushed battering rams up the ramp to breach the wall of the fortress.

Refusing to be captured or killed by the Romans, the zealots cast lots to pick ten men who acted as executioners of every man, woman, and child, and then they too killed themselves.

Today many new recruits of the (IDF) Israeli Defense Forces march to the top of Masada to receive their coveted green berets.

Masada is a symbol of courage, character, and endless determination. The former IDF commander Moshe Dayan initiated the practice of holding the swearing-in ceremony at Masada for various units of the IDF. The symbolism of Masada continues to resonate in modern Israel; the refrain that "Masada shall not fall again" is still heard today.

For today's men who seek adventure, the story of the siege of Masada may inspire images of action, passion, courage and sacrifice; virtues that every man yearns for.

CHARACTER BUILDERS

God calls men to be, "A Rock in Hard Places." For many of us, that message reinforces the need for men to be men. Our society tries to feminize men and boys to the detriment of the church.

Men were created to be protectors, providers and warriors. When men shrink back from their God-given purpose, the church suffers. The church needs strong, godly men who passionately serve God under the authority of a Bible believing local church.

The sad truth is that today's men do not have many opportunities to show courage or sacrifice. Sure, it takes courage to stand up to your boss, who may be a jerk, and family priorities may require you to sacrifice your free time, but real times of action, courage, and sacrifice are hard to come by. That's why it's so important to carve out times of adventure.

In our materialistic society, many men find adventure in their work. There's nothing wrong with working hard. Work is honorable, but work and career shouldn't take the place of time in the wilderness.

David Roth of Work Matters, a workplace ministry located in Fayetteville, Arkansas, encourages believers like Donnie Smith, CEO of Tyson Foods, to see the workplace as a mission field. Smith recently shared how his work has become more rewarding, and he has become more passionate because of this mission-minded outlook. He told of how God has made him more sensitive to the needs and hurts among employees he meets. He now takes more time to listen and is more symphonic to people. So, in some respects, work is an adventure.

THE ADVENTURE EVANGELIST

If today's business heroes are adventure capitalist, then surely the Apostle Paul was the first "Adventure Evangelist." Pauls' day job was as a tentmaker and the theme of Paul's long-running series would have been, "Everything ventured, everything gained." Paul had an unstoppable passion to carry out the mission God had given him.

In Philippians 1:21 Paul say, "For me, to live is Christ, to die is gain." He meant Christ was with him now in life, but it would be even better to be with Him when he went to heaven.

Taking this little analogy one step further, Paul's go-go gear was the full armor of God. He was clothed in righteousness; he had put on the new self. The Holy Spirit of the Living God had transformed Paul.

In his book "The Apostle; The Life of Paul," author John Pollock paints a vivid picture of Paul's adventures. Hiking through rugged mountains, crossing roaring rivers, facing hunger and loneliness, Paul endured.

Pure adventure for some is taking God's word to a lost world. Paul was beaten, shipwrecked, stoned, and imprisoned, yet he says in 2 Corinthians 5:14, "The love of God compels us." Paul could do nothing less than carry out the adventure God had called him to.

The entire Book of Acts is an adventure story with risk, danger, exotic locations, villains and Kings. Paul's missionary journey takes the reader on a thrilling expedition of life and death.

Another example of pure adventure is my friend Jeff Schmidt whose passion for the lost compelled him to pack up everything he owns and move his family to Tanzania. Jeff was convinced God was calling him to full time missions in Africa. Jeff's ministry, *His Water International,* drills water wells in the remote villages of southeastern Africa. He spent months raising the necessary funds to purchase the well drilling equipment and shipping it to Africa.

A rugged faith, a determined call to go, pushes men like Jeff to strike out and build a ministry, which brings hope and a future to the people of Tanzania.

Jeff relates a story of how he came to this adventurous life. "I was sitting in a village meeting with about 40 Muslim men, just passed us were 60 or 70 women sitting altogether. There were also dozens of children playing just beyond them. The men pointed out the problem they had in their village with the lack of water, it was a desperate problem. For over 800 people in the village the only fresh water was a spring about the size of a 5-gallon bucket. The spring was only about 4 inches deep and was in the mud flat of the ocean. When the tide came in they had no fresh water, only when the tide receded did it reveal the spring and they were able to get semi-fresh water.

Schmidt continues, "We began visiting the village twice a week. We started teaching English and developing relationships. During this time I was raising funds to help their village and 11 months later we were able to drill the well in the village and begin to pump clean water for the first time. As I looked at the faces of the people I saw the excitement and anticipation in their eyes. It was at this moment I realized I had to do this for the rest of my life! Helping villages with water problems opens the door to share the gospel of Jesus Christ. I believe God had been preparing me for this adventure my whole life."

Adventure is important to men; a shared wilderness experience is something deeply satisfying. Someone has even gone so far as to

ADVENTURE WITH A PURPOSE

establish October 14th as, "National Day of Adventure." Opportunities for action, courage, and sacrifice bring meaning and purpose into a man's life.

One old explorer, when asked why he endured the cold, wet, and hunger of long expeditions, said, "I went along to iron the wrinkles out of my soul."

HARD CORE ADVENTURE BUILDS CHARACTER

The extreme sports movement is hot today. Base jumping off cliffs or buildings, skydiving, challenge-endurance races, long-distance bike racing, wing-suit flying, and rock climbing, just to mention a few.

Dubbed "Joe Hardcore," by Men's Journal, Joe De Sena created the Spartan Race in 2004. The Spartan Race is one of most popular events for those who want the extreme challenge. Spartan is a series of obstacles of varying distance and difficulty. Obstacles can include a fire jump, crawling under barbed wire, wall climbing, and mud crawling. Other intense events like rope climb, heavy object carries, bouldering wall and rope swing.

Other extreme sports groups include Tough Mudder, Warrior Dash, and Rugged Maniac. Here's how Rugged Maniac issues a challenge, "You could spend your Saturday running errands or binge-watching TV, but wouldn't it be more fun to do something absolutely insane with your friends!"

Why do some men gravitate toward these extreme adventures? "There's an innate characteristic in some people," says Justin Anderson, PHD, a sports consultant for the Center for Sports Psychology in Denton, Texas. "Some people are turned on by that stuff; they get a lot of adrenaline by it, and they gravitate toward activities that give them that feeling.

For some it's jumping out of airplanes, for others its climbing Mt. Everest, and for others, it's the Ironman. When they find that sport or activity that gives them that feeling, they say there is nothing better."

While reaching their goal, or winning a competition can be their reasons for involvement in extreme sports, "A lot of extreme athletes report that they are seeking that rush," says Anderson. "They're looking for those sensations they get from putting their life on the line."

Some feel that men who are involved in extreme sports are reckless and seeking something to fill a void in their lives that only God can fill. In the book "Deliverance," Lewis, the Burt Reynolds character, is described this way, "Lewis wanted to be immortal. He had everything that life could give, and couldn't make it work."

Pastor John Piper's book "Risk: Better to Lose Your Life Than to Waste It" addresses the extreme sport craze. He says, "We must examine the motive for risk. Is the risk to exalt one's self, perhaps to make you feel superior to others, or is it a reckless lust for danger?" Piper goes on to point out, "The Christian life is a call to risk." In Luke 21:16 we see that some will risk death, "You will even be betrayed by parents, brothers, relatives, and friends. They will kill some of you."

Again in I. Peter 4:12 we see this risk of following Christ, "Dear friends, don't be surprised when the fiery ordeal comes among you to test you as if something unusual were happening to you."

Piper nails it when he says, "Our risk is the means by which we show the value of Christ. Showing love to our enemies despite the risk stuns a pagan world."

GET IN THE GAME
"Expedition Unknown, Forged in Fire, Live Free or Die, Mountain Men, Extreme Off-Road, and Alaska the Last Frontier," these are TV shows I would call "adventure reality shows."

It's much easier to watch other people's adventures than have your own. No sweat, no expense, other than the cable bill. We get fat and lazy, as we convince ourselves that this is a cool adventure. Have we lost our passion, have we become a spectator nation? Per a recent study, 42% of Americans can't remember the last time they had attempted an adventure.

Don't get me wrong, I love all these shows, but it's not the same as being there. Compared to the feel of soft pine needles underfoot on a morning hike, or the smell of honeysuckle and cedar as you approach a mountain lake. Reality outdoors just can't compare to the real thing.

God has placed natural beauty all around us for our enjoyment. There's nothing more beautiful than a sunset over the Pacific Ocean, or the snowcapped mountains reflected in a clear Colorado lake.

DEAD SEA ADVENTURES
The Judean Wilderness of Israel occupies the area from the eastern slopes of the Judea Mountains down to the Great Rift Valley, and runs along the western shore of the Dead Sea.

Leaving the mountain fortress of Masada we began a descent along the west side of the Dead Sea. Following Israel Highway 90, the lowest road in the world, we are at -1,400 below sea level when we reach the Dead Sea.

It's nearing dark and the crowds are beginning to drift away from the shoreline. After some discussion, we decide to set up camp on the sandy beach. The air is super dry with a distinctive salt odor. The surprising chill of the night air sends me looking for my windbreaker.

Before turning in for the night, we visit a small café/store just up the beach and treat ourselves to ice cream. Sitting on the sand staring through the eerie haze we can make out the rocky, treeless mountains of the nation of Jordan across the water.

Unbeknownst to us at the time, only a few miles west of us, is what Backpacker Magazine calls, "The World's Unlikeliest Trail." The Abraham Path is a relatively new hiking trail funded and developed by donations from the World Bank. This West Bank, Palestinian controlled, section of the trail stretches 185 miles from Hebron in the south to Jenin in the north. George Rishmawi, Director of this section of The Abraham Path in Palestine, sees the path as a way to help Palestinians embrace their history, appreciate the land, and escape the strict, confinements of the West Bank. About two million foreign tourists visited the West Bank last year with the West Bank cities of Bethlehem and Jericho getting most of the tourist for day visits. Only about 6,000 people have hiked the new trail.

The new trail is named after Abraham whose role in this land is enormous; he is known as the father of the three major religions of the world, Christianity, Islam and Judaism. In this divided land, perhaps spending time along the Jesus Trail and the Abraham Path can help bring adventure loving people together, if only for a day or two.

PURE OUTREACH

Adventure can often bring people together for shared experiences. Many churches are turning to outdoor ministry as an outreach to non-believers.

Wild Game Dinners, and Outdoor Expo's are becoming annual events at many churches. Liberty University and Thomas Road Baptist Church in Lynchburg, Virginia host "Wildfire and Ignite." These weekend events point toward reaching the sportsman. The events features nationally known guest speakers, outdoor gear exhibitors, and a wild game dinner.

Second Baptist Church in Conway, Arkansas hosts "Beast Feast," one of the largest wild game dinners in the nation. My friend Scottie

Johnson uses this event to steer men to his Outdoor Church of Arkansas. Our Rugged Faith Ministries hosts "Rugged Faith Boot Camp' for men who love the outdoors.

Many families are turning to adventure to create lasting memories. Guided tours are not my thing. I'm much more of a plan-it-yourself person, but there are many excellent guided adventures for families. Conquering outdoor challenges is a great way to draw families closer together and build your kids confidence levels. Mountain biking, hiking or backpacking is always a good choice for families, and kayaking and canoeing for the water lovers.

Jim Potts, owner of Lewis and Clark Outfitters in Rogers, Arkansas tells me that camping is the outdoor adventure his family most loved. When the weekend came, the family would toss their tents and sleeping bags in the car and set out for one of the numerous lakes or streams that dot the mountains of the Ozarks.

Potts recalls, his now adult boys still laugh about the time he chose an awesome looking campsite on the banks of a clear mountain stream in southern Missouri, only to be awakened in the middle of the night by three inches of water coming into their tent. Potts smiles, "Maybe that's why that awesome camp site had been vacant on a holiday weekend."

Loren Siekman of Pure Adventures is also a huge advocate for family adventure. He says, "In our day-to-day lives, it's often challenging to get everyone in a family together at the same time. With everyone so busy with work, school, sports, and hobbies it often seems impossible to coordinate schedules and spend quality time as a family."

Finding family adventure is not difficult. Making the time and doing it is the challenge. Trust me when I say, you will not regret time spent in the wilderness with your family. The memories you make are golden. Start with something as simple as planning a Saturday morning hike with the family or with members of your small group at church. Maybe it could involve un-churched friends and neighbors who might be hesitant to attend church but would be excited about a short-term adventure with friends.

"TRAIL THOUGHT #5"
What are you passionate about and how can you utilize that passion to benefit others and to glorify God?

6

LEADERSHIP LESSONS ...PROBLEM SOLVER

ONE IMPORTANT ELEMENT of outdoor adventure is that it forces us to be better decision-makers, and problem-solvers. We must prepare before we go. We must adjust our plans and remain flexible, and we must build bridges of trust with those whom we travel.

On day eight we headed north from Galilee toward the Jordan River. The Jordan is the life-blood of the nation of Israel. Flowing 156 miles from its source near Mount Hermon, four streams gather to form the Jordan before it reaches the Sea of Galilee.

We walked to the midpoint of the Arik Bridge, which crosses the Jordan River just north of the Sea of Galilee. The narrow wooden span was an important strategic point during Israel's 1973 Yom Kippur War with its Arab neighbors.

Mike and Bill, our military history experts, shared their wisdom of the fascinating story of the Bailey bridges. An English civil engineer, Sir Donald Bailey, invented the Bailey bridge in 1942. The bridges were portable, pre-fab, truss bridges, and required no special tools or heavy equipment to construct. The wood and steel bridges were small and light enough to be carried on trucks and lifted into place by hand. English Field Marshall Montgomery said, "Without the Bailey Bridge, we could not have won World War II." Two of these simple Bailey bridges still remain in use today in Israel. As we stood on one of those bridges called "The Bridge of the Daughters of Jacob," we were all moved by the sacrifices of those who defended this sacred land.

As it meanders southward, the Jordan is deep and muddy at this point. In times of war, I can certainly see the value of having portable bridges to quickly span this important waterway.

We were not able to spend as much time along the Jordan as I would have wished, so much to see, yet so little time. On my next trip to Israel I hope to visit the traditional site where John the Baptist baptized Jesus, or kayak a portion of the waters of the Jordan.

The Jordan River has become a symbol of entering the Promised Land. "Crossing Over Jordan', or fording the Jordan remains a timeless metaphor for crossing over from death to life. Hebrews 4:1-10 says, "For the person who has entered His rest has rested from his own works, just as God did from His." In Joshua Chapter 3:1-17 we find the story of the Israelites entering the land which God had promised their forefathers.

Leadership lessons learned in the outdoors can be inter-woven into life lessons. Read the below passage carefully, and then I want to point out some interesting leadership lessons I have learned from Joshua.

JOSHUA CHAPTER 3:1-17

1"Joshua started early the next morning and left the Acacia Grove with all the Israelites. They went as far as the Jordan and stayed there before crossing. **2** After three days the officers went through the camp **3** and commanded the people: "When you see the ark of the covenant of the Lord your God carried by the Levitical priests, you must break camp and follow it. **4** But keep a distance of about 1,000 yards between yourselves and the ark. Don't go near it, so that you can see the way to go, for you haven't traveled this way before.

5 Joshua told the people, "Consecrate yourselves, because the Lord will do wonders among you tomorrow. **6** Then he said to the priests, "Take the Ark of the Covenant and go on ahead of the people." So, they carried the Ark of the Covenant and went ahead of them.

7 The Lord spoke to Joshua: "Today I will begin to exalt you in the sight of all Israel, so they will know that I will be with you just as I was with Moses. **8** Command the priests carrying the Ark of the Covenant: When you reach the edge of the waters, stand in the Jordan."

9 Then Joshua told the Israelites, "Come closer and listen to the words of the Lord your God." **10** He said: "You will know that the living God is among you and that He will certainly dispossess before you the Canaanites, Hittites, Hivites, Perizzites, Girgashites, Amorites, and Jebusites **11** when the ark of the covenant of the Lord of all the earth goes ahead of you into the Jordan.

12 Now choose 12 men from the tribes of Israel, one man for each tribe. **13** When the feet of the priests who carry the ark of the Lord, the Lord of all the earth, come to rest in the Jordan's waters, its waters will be cut off. The water flowing downstream will stand up in a mass."

14 When the people broke camp to cross the Jordan, the priests carried the Ark of the Covenant ahead of the people. **15** Now the Jordan overflows its banks throughout the harvest season. But as soon as the priests carrying the ark reached the Jordan, their feet touched the water at its edge **16** and the water flowing downstream stood still, rising in a mass that extended as far as Adam, a city next to Zarethan.

The water flowing downstream into the Sea of the Arabah (the Dead Sea) was completely cut off, and the people crossed opposite Jericho.

17 The priests carrying the Ark of the Lord's covenant stood firmly on dry ground in the middle of the Jordan, while all Israel crossed on dry ground until the entire nation had finished crossing the Jordan."

I love the description by Pastor Lloyd Stilley, "As they approached the famous river that formed a barrier between them and their longed-for real estate, what they saw by the light of day was both confusing and dreadful. The Jordan was defiantly uncrossable!"

There's a simple sentence in v. 15 that gives us the picture: "Now the Jordan overflows its banks throughout the harvest season." The gentle Jordan was now a raging river, swelled to flood stage. Currents can reach up to 40-miles an hour when the Jordan floods. What is more, the plain that surrounds this river was packed with tangled brush and dense growth."

Jeremiah the prophet mentions the thickets of the Jordan River in Jeremiah 12:5. One writer said, "It was not the river so much as the jungle that was difficult to cross."

The Jordan had swelled its banks, spreading about a mile across, ranging in depth from 3 feet to 12 feet, all covering thick undergrowth. What is God teaching us in this story?

I pray this message will offer you valuable leadership insight from God's Word.

THE 10 LEADERSHIP LESSONS FROM JOSHUA

1. <u>Great leaders start their day early</u>. Notice in verse 1, "Joshua started early the next morning," Before others rise, while it's still and quiet, for me this is the best time of the day. King David, In Psalm 119:147 says, "I rise before the dawn and cry for help, I wait for your words."

In Mark 1:35 we see where the world's best leader started early, "In the early morning, while it was still dark, Jesus got up, left the house, and went away to a secluded place, and was praying there."

Another noted leader was Abraham, "Now Abraham arose early in the morning and went to the place where he had stood before the LORD' Genesis 19:27. Great leaders begin their day early.

2. <u>Great Leaders Stop and Pray before making Major Decisions</u>. In verses 2 and 3 Joshua stopped for three days before crossing the Jordan River.

I don't believe they needed to rest, the walk from Acacia Grove to the river's edge is an easy one, and it's just a few miles over smooth ground. I believe Joshua was waiting to hear from the Lord. When in doubt, don't forge ahead, stop and pray for direction.

This was a major decision, which affected thousands of people. Joshua stopped. Do you stop whenever you come to the edge of substantial choices?

On our hike along the Jesus Trail, in one Arab village we were forced to make a choice. As I mentioned earlier we had encountered some small boys who tried to stone us. A potentially more dangerous obstacle followed this mostly harmless incident. Bill had scouted ahead and discovered a group of older teens a few hundred yards ahead in our projected path. After some discussion, Bill and Mike made the decision that we should alter our route to avoid any potential confrontation.

Stop and pray before making major decisions.

3. <u>Great Leaders train their team</u>. Joshua had developed a team around him just as Moses had. In verse 2 we see that Joshua shared the mission with his officers then sent them throughout the camp to instruct the people.

One of the primary responsibilities of a leader is to build a great team and train them to carry out your vision for the church, or organization.

The officers, staff, and managers of your organization should be so well versed in the leaders' vision that they can give specific instructions to the people under their direction. I will paraphrase here; notice the officers said, "When you see the ark move, you move."

Great leaders are great teachers. Train your team.

4. <u>Great Leaders ask for a Commitment</u>. Few leaders can accomplish major tasks without the buy-in from their followers. Here in verse 5, Joshua asks for a commitment from the people. He says, "Consecrate yourselves." Basically, he asked the people, "Will you dedicate yourselves, because God requires it?"

Joshua was saying to the people, "We have been at this for forty years in the wilderness, you know what God requires, are you willing to do it?"

Consecrate means, "The separation of oneself from things that are unclean, especially anything that would contaminate one's relationship with a perfect God."

Leaders! Don't be afraid to ask for a commitment. Tell people the truth; share the risks as well as potential rewards. Be bold in the Lord, he will bless your striving for holiness.

5. <u>Great Leaders are motivators</u>. You don't have to be a ra' ra' guy to be a great motivator. Some of our best leaders have been quiet and low key, even introverts.

In verse 5 Joshua firsts instructs the people to consecrate themselves, then he speaks to inspire, to encourage them. He says, "The Lord will work wonders among you tomorrow."

Joshua wasn't just blowing smoke like some modern day motivational speaker; he knew the people had witnessed God's wonders over the past forty years. They had seen God provide food and water; they had seen mighty works of God.

Great Christian leaders are motivated by their love for God and for people. Their zeal and passion comes from knowing that God wants the best for them and for those they lead.

6. <u>Great Leaders Anticipate Great Things Happening</u>. Pray expecting God to answer. It's a faith issue. Anticipate God doing great things. Remember times when God has answered your prayers.

Confidence in God is not based on a worldly hope, but on God's promises that are true. Our hope is in Jesus. Joshua was not "hoping we make it across the river." No, Joshua was sure of God's provision, he was anticipating God to work mighty wonders just has He had done in the past.

7. <u>Great Leaders Always Place God First</u>. The Ark of the Covenant contained the glory of God. It was the presence of God with the people of Israel.

Notice in verses 6-7-8 Joshua instructed the priest who carried the Ark of the Covenant to lead out. "Take the Ark of the Covenant and go before the people."

When you follow God, you can become a great leader. One thing I have learned over the past ten years of ministry is to stay in God's shadow. Let him lead. I have seen it happen to others and I have experiences in our ministry; put God first, stay in His shadow. Great leaders follow their King.

8. <u>Great Leaders Stay close to their People</u>. The old adage "They don't care how much you know, until they know how much you care," is overused but so true. People follow leaders they like and respect.

In verse 9 Joshua tells the Israelites, "Come closer and listen to the words of the Lord your God." Joshua is telling them to bend an ear, this is important, or as Pastor Andy Stanley encourages, "Lean into leaders."

How does a leader stay connected to his people? This is often difficult for leaders like myself who are natural introverts. I sometimes find myself more focused on the process of ministry, than on the people.

Leaders who love their people can overcome a lot of problems because unity grows as a leader serves his followers.

9. <u>Great Leaders Delegate</u>. This leadership lesson is closely related to lesson number three concerning training your team. Great leaders surround themselves with great people who have bought into their leadership style and vision. Thus, the leader can be confident that when he needs to delegate a task, it will be handled much like he would handle it himself.

Joshua followed the example his mentor Moses had taught him. In verse 12 Joshua tells the people, "Now choose 12 men from the tribes of Israel, one man for each tribe."

Moses had modeled this skill of delegation over forty years ago; Joshua gleaned valuable leadership lessons from one of the greatest leaders of all time.

10. <u>Great Leaders Overcome Obstacles</u> The Jordan River was an important boundary to be crossed. It stood between the Israelites and the land God had promised their ancestors. Even at flood stage it was no match for the Living God.

The Jordan River also represents a decision point in our lives, a point of transition. Great leaders overcome obstacles. Helping others to bridge that great rift caused by their sinful nature, which keeps them from reaching the Promised Land.

Once again I quote Pastor Stilley, "So many of us face Personal Jordan's that feel so permanent and powerful that we don't even try to make it across. Our lives feel stalled, stuck on the wrong side of God's promises."

As we stand on the brink of the God-sized future and consider the obstacles that hinder us, it can feel like we're facing an impossible task between here and there. Your big obstacles may seem uncrossable, but take heart they are no match for the Way-Maker. He knows how to get you to the other side

"TRAIL THOUGHT #6"

Consider people you know who are bridge-builders, and way-makers. What is it about their life that is different from yours? What aspects would you like to emulate in your own life?

7

DISCOVERY ...RISK

DISCOVERY REQUIRES A certain amount of risk. Doug Coupland says, "Adventure without risk is Disneyland." The challenge of overcoming risk and danger is part of the appeal of adventure. Risk and discovery are companions, one always pushing the other to new heights.

In his articles entitled "Micro-Adventures," author Alastair Humphreys says, "I wanted to see what was out there. I wanted to do something hard and stupid. I wanted to see if I could handle it. Above all, I wanted freedom, escape, and all the delicious, unknown possibilities of discovery."

Childhood can be our first age of discovery. As a child, I remember reading a series of adventure books entitled "We Were There," children's novels retelling historical events and featuring one or more kids as the primary characters.

There were exciting titles such as "We Were There at the Alamo, We Were There with the Pony Express, and We Were There on the Oregon Trail." But my all-time favorite was the 1959 classic "We Were There with Lewis & Clark" by James Munves.

At age 12 or 13, when I first read these books, I was in the boat, and then on the trail with Captains Meriwether Lewis and William Clark. In my mind, I was wearing the coonskin cap and the fringe buckskins, carrying my Kentucky long rifle, risking it all to reach the Pacific.

I have never lost my fascination with explorers like Lewis and Clark. To this day, I love to read their handwritten journals and visit remote sites along their 2,400-mile route from St Louis, Missouri to Astoria, Oregon.

I'm planning a trip to explore a section of the trail in southern Montana and eastern Idaho. The Lolo Trail follows the original route of Lewis and Clark and stretches about 120 miles across the Bitterroot Mountains west of Lolo, Montana to just east of Kamiah, Idaho. Our adventure will take us along a primitive dirt road, known as the Lolo Motorway, or Forest Service Road 500. Instead of walking as Lewis and Clark did in September 1805, we will be riding Honda 4-wheelers in June of 2017.

I believe the idea of a group of men risking discomfort and even death, striking out across a vast unknown to explore wild and mysterious places, appeals to most men, even those who might not consider themselves outdoorsmen. Adventure, discovery, and exploration seem to be embedded in a man's DNA. Risk, danger and action are, for many men, necessary ingredients to a full and meaningful life.

DESERT DISCOVERIES

From day one, and throughout our Jesus Trail adventure, exploring historical sites was a major emphasis of our time in Israel. Mike and Bill, our two archeology buffs, took us to several sites of ancient biblical ruins.

For Christians, Israel is a special place of discovery. We wanted to get to know the people as best we could: their foods, customs, likes, dislikes, fears, and dreams. Our plan was to experience as much as possible in the time we had. We wanted to hike, climb, float, swim, feel, touch and smell the place called Israel.

Tels, as they are called, offer wonderful insight into stories found in Scripture. A Tel is a mound where a city once existed. After a city was destroyed, new inhabits would rebuild on the same spot, creating layer after layer of civilizations. Today many of the Tels are being excavated, and artifacts being discovered are shedding new light on what life was life in ancient Israel.

From Tel Megiddo, Tel Dan, Tel Hazor, Tel Lakish, to Tel Arad, we made new discoveries at each stop. Seeing an ancient stone version of a mercy seat, like the ones described in Exodus, viewing a primitive wine press, like those mentioned in the New Testament, and exploring the remains of a Solomon gate, were all faith-building experiences, which come through discovery.

In the back of this book (Appendix-D) you will find a more in-depth description of the Biblical Archaeology's Top Ten Discoveries of 2015 from Christianity Today.

CORPS OF DISCOVERY

In 1803 Lewis and Clark were chosen by President Thomas Jefferson to lead an expedition to explore and map the newly acquired area known as the Louisiana Purchase.

Lewis and Clark then chose 33 U.S. Army volunteers and experienced frontiersmen to make up the Corps of Discovery.

The Corps departed from St. Louis, Missouri on May 21, 1804. They traveled in a 55-foot custom-built Keelboat and two 35-foot long pirogues, or canoe-type boats.

The boats were loaded with supplies, including food, gun powder, weapons, gifts for the Indians they would meet, and hundreds of other items.

The mission of the Corps of Discovery was to explore the land and map the physical terrain, while searching for a possible water route to the Pacific Ocean.

Jefferson gave them authority to establish an American presence in this vast area and stake claim to its natural resources, while contacting the native Indian tribes in the area.

Stephen Ambrose, in his excellent book on Lewis and Clark entitled, "Undaunted Courage," spends a lot of time discussing the meticulous preparation Meriwether Lewis took before they set off into the wilderness.

Ambrose's book has a complete list of supplies and gear purchased by Lewis and Clark. He also goes to great lengths to describe the struggles the group encountered during their two years in the wilderness.

The Journals of Lewis and Clark, plus those of a few other members so the Corps of Discovery also bring to life the day-to-day obstacles the group faced.

Every mile was a challenge as they encountered obstacles such as inhospitable weather, flooded rivers, wild animals, hostile Indians, and swarms of mosquitoes.

The cost of the Corps of Discovery's two-year expedition was about $2,500 for the initial list of supplies and gear, and an additional $39,000, using a letter of credit that Jefferson provided him. That was a lot in money in 1800!

As far as human costs, only one member of the Corps of Discovery died on the trip. Sergeant Charles Floyd died in 1804, most likely a result of a burst appendix.

DISCOVER THE BITTERROOTS

Forest Service Road 500 is a narrow, twisty ribbon carved across the Bitterroot Mountains by Civilian Conservation Corps workers in the 1930's. We plan to pick our way around jagged rocks and deep ruts, which closely followed the Lewis and Clark Trail.

Our Honda 4-wheelers will be loaded with gear and fuel needed to complete the three-day trek along the Lolo Trail. The plan is to ride west, stopping at the historical markers found along the trail, and spend two nights of primitive camping. For about 125 miles, Highway 12 follows Lolo Creek, Lochsa River, the Clearwater River and Selway River, through rugged and spectacular sections of Montana and Idaho. We are already planning to make this an annual adventure.

Perhaps the key point of any expedition is what will we do with the discoveries we make. Will we sit on them, keeping the treasure to ourselves, or will we tell the world? I believe discoveries are useless until they are shared.

In 1806 many thought mountain man John Colter was crazy when he told them he had found a place in the Rocky Mountains with boiling mud pots and giant geysers spraying into the air. They call it "Colter's Hell." Colter was on the return trip with Lewis and Clark when he came across an area, which today is thought to be Yellowstone National Park in Wyoming.

What if Colter had kept silent, avoided the ridicule, and kept his discovery to himself? Certainly, others would have discovered it later and gotten the credit, but Colter would have missed the real blessing and excitement, which comes when discoveries are shared.

It's the same with discoveries we find hidden in the pages of God's word. Until we share what we have found, it's simply ink on a page. In Matthew 5:15-17 Jesus commands us to be a light to the world. "No one lights a lamp and hides it under a basket."

Author Bruce Feiler says, "The way to keep a trail alive is to walk on it." God's story, the Gospel trail, must be used, and shared with others to keep it alive." What would happen if everyone stopped hike the Jesus Trail or the Appalachian Trail? They would become overgrown and eventually disappear.

DISCOVER BIBLICAL TRUTH

I find many parallels to the mission of Lewis and Clark and the Great Commission found in Mathew 28. As Christians, our King has chosen us. As David Murrow says, "He left us a dangerous and demanding mission." We are God's hands and feet on this earth, and we have been given the Holy Spirit as a helper in our mission to spread the gospel of Jesus Christ.

Our mission is to explore God's Word, in order that we may discover the truths of God. These truths can lead us down the path to the abundant life with Christ, to access the vast spiritual wealth found in a close personal relationship with Almighty God, and to establish meaningful relationships with other people so they might come to know God.

While in Israel, I rediscovered why our mission as Christians is so critical to a dying world. Standing on the hill at Tel Megiddo, overlooking the valley below, I was reminded of how Revelation 19 prophesies this valley location for a final battle of Armageddon during the end times. Seeing this place in person heightened the stark realization that millions of people are spiritually lost and will spend eternity separated from God unless we follow the mission Jesus gave us.

The Bible is a book of discovery. Unlike a GPS, which must be updated, the Bible is a map that never goes out of date. As we mine the depths of God's Word we discover life-changing truths and wisdom. The book of Jeremiah shows us God's love is unfailing, "I have loved you with an everlasting love." Another discovery can be found in James 1:17, concerning God's unchangeable character, "Every good and perfect gift is from above, coming down from the Father of the heavenly lights, who does not change like shifting shadows."

Explore the mysteries of God's Word, and you will find a vast, untamed, mind-altering expanse just waiting to be discovered. The biblical truths we discover build our faith and draw us closer to God. These discoveries may come rapidly, or after long periods of silence. It all depends on our willingness and our ability to explore.

3 Common Ingredients of All Successful Expeditions

All successful expeditions have three common ingredients: a person, a plan, and a place. Expeditions do not happen in a vacuum, some Person has a burning desire to explore some untamed, or uncharted place. As time passes, this desire grows, as the idea marinates in their mind. This person may share his vision with others to get advice, or they may guard it out of fear another will beat him to the goal or dissuade him. The person who has the vision is the first of these common ingredients. Without a vision, nothing happens.

Once the time is right and the leader has accessed the challenge, he begins to develop a Plan of how to get there. This plan is very important to the success of the expedition. The old Army saying, "Proper planning prevents poor performance" is certainly true. The plan will include needed resources, an estimate of time required and an assessment of possible obstacles to success. The better the plan, the greater odds of success.

Once the plan is complete, the <u>Place</u> becomes the focus. All that remains is to go, "just do it," as Nike says; sometimes alone, but usually with a group. Many expeditions fail due to poor leadership, poor planning, or failure to recognize the effort required to reach the destination.

These same three elements can be found in a spiritual expedition. The Christian life is a journey. The person is you and me. God draws us to seek to know Him better. The plan is found in the Gospels and throughout the Bible, and the place is eternity with God in Heaven. It's God expedition, He created it, He is the guide, He is finisher, and He is the destination.

Expeditions of discovery and our spiritual journey both have other common elements, such as avoiding and overcoming obstacles, surrounding ourselves with people who enhance our chance of success, and daily discipline to continue.

RISKS VS. DISCOVERY

As we think about discovery and adventure in the Christian life, and the common ingredients involved in discovery, what obstacles do we face? What are the costs of following our King, and what are the costs of failing to follow Jesus? Lets' look at an example found in God's Word.

In the Old Testament, we find the story of Moses, Joshua, Caleb, and the twelve spies. In Numbers 13 we see obstacles, one of the common ingredient of any adventure. We also see the terrible consequences when God's people fail to follow His direction.

Moses sent the twelve spies into the Promised Land. After forty days, they returned with a mixed report. The many obstacles they found were reported in two very different ways.

Joshua and Caleb tell the people, "We must go up and take possession of the land because we can certainly conquer it!" But, the other ten spies tell a different story. The ten doubting spies say, "The people living in the land are strong, and the cities are large and fortified. We can't go up against the people because they are stronger than we are!"

Because of the bad report of the ten, the people rebelled against Moses' leadership, and against God's plan. Consider for a moment what might have been if the people had sided with Moses, Joshua, Caleb instead of the ten doubters.

The discovery the spies made was as God had promised, a land flowing with milk and honey. Ten of the twelve spies were fearful; the risk was not worth the reward. The results of their rebellion were devastating, as a whole generation of Israelites died in the wilderness, never to see the Promised Land.

Joshua and Caleb were forced to wander in the wilderness for forty years because of the people's fear and doubt, and tragically, Moses was kept from entering the Promised Land at this time, because of the people's disobedience.

Obstacles, such as risk, fear of the unknown, and doubt, can also create hardships for us as they did for the wandering Israelites. Many times, these negative forces can be overcome through prayer and the power of the Holy Spirit.

We must also do our part to overcome risk, fear, and doubt. In her great new book author Amy Morin has discovered the following "13 Actions that Mentally Tough People Don't Do."

1. They don't waste time feeling sorry for themselves.
2. They don't give away their power by failing to forgive.

3. They don't shy away from change
4. They don't focus on things they can't control
5. They don't worry about pleasing everyone
6. They don't fear taking calculated risks
7. They don't dwell on the past
8. They don't make the same mistakes over and over
9. They don't resent other people's success
10. They don't give up after the first failure
11. They don't fear alone time
12. They don't feel the world owes them anything
13. They don't expect immediate results

TRAIL DISCOVERIES

Meanwhile, back on the Lolo Trail. If all goes as planned we will make our way along the Lolo Trail in southern Montana in the coming months. We plan to make camp at Traveler's Rest, located about a mile south of Lolo, Montana where the Lolo Creek joins the Bitterroot River. Lewis and Clark camped here in September 1805, before crossing into what's now the state of Idaho. The Corps acquired as many horses as possible and enlisted the help of a member of the Shoshone nation known as Old Toby.

To get through the more than 156-mile stretch of unforgiving mountain terrain, they followed the Lolo Trail for eleven harrowing days suffering from frostbite, malnutrition and dehydration, and near starvation.

For Lewis and Clark, this was perhaps the most difficult portion of the entire expedition. Studying the Topo maps of the backbone of the Bitterroots, I can see why! Steep, dusty, and rocky, with thick forest and dense undergrowth, I can only imagine having to traverse this on foot, following nothing more than wild game trails.

Experiencing the rugged terrain while hiking the Jesus Trail, and exploring lands of the Bible, produced a broader understanding and awe for what our heroes of the faith endured.

During Day seven of the Jesus Trail trip, we visited one of the most beautiful places in all of Israel, the ancient city of Caesarea on the Mediterranean Sea; not to be confused with Caesarea Philippi, which is in the Golan Heights area of northern Israel.

We walked the ruins of Herod the Great's elaborate complex, which includes a 3,500-seat theater, ruins of an Olympic-size swimming pool, administrative quarters, and statues; all on the edge of a magnificent man-made harbor. Exploring further, we discovered a series of well-preserved aqueducts extending along the coast. They were used to bring water from the base of Mount Carmel, nearly ten miles away!

This city was home to Cornelius, the first Gentile convert in Acts 10:1, and was also home to Philip the evangelist. Pontius Pilate lived here and served as a provincial governor.

In Acts 23 we find the story of the Apostle Paul being imprisoned at Caesarea. Remains of the jail cell still exist. The story continues in Acts 26 as Paul is being brought before King Agrippa at the palace in Caesarea. This is one of the most awesome accounts found anywhere for speaking truth to power. I encourage you to re-read this chapter in Acts and be inspired by Paul's courage, as he defends himself, and shares the Gospel of Jesus with King Agrippa and his court.

Paul's missionary journeys to the remote mountain cities and towns of modern day Turkey, Greece, Crete, Lebanon, Syria, and Macedonia were adventures with a purpose. After his dramatic conversion on the road to Damascus, Paul was a man on a mission. He was certain God had called him to take the message of Christianity to the Gentiles.

Around 44 A.D. Paul and Barnabas, along with John Mark, set out from Antioch, Syria. This first missionary journey took Paul to

Cyprus, then into the folds of the Toros Mountains in Turkey. In Acts 13:13 we find that John Mark, for some unknown reason, left them and went back to Jerusalem

Upon leaving Cyprus, Paul and Barnabas went into the heart of Anatolia, choosing the treacherous path through Perga to Pisidian Antioch, hiking through dangerous mountains and stunning scenery.

Paul and Barnabas could have taken an easy path along established Roman roads, but opted to travel along the rugged Kestros Valley, most likely because of the hospitality of local Jewish communities.

Today you can follow in the footsteps of Paul by trekking the Saint Paul Trail, a well-marked 300-mile trail that begins near Perga, in southern Turkey, and extends into the mountains of Turkey.

Adventure is everywhere, waiting to be discovered and experienced. You may find it in the pages of the history of Lewis and Clark, or on the pages of the Bible.

Discovery requires action and involves risk. We must take the initiative to dream, weigh the risks, then to go. I pray that you will discover the awesome wonders of God's creation today as you explore the great outdoors and as you explore God's Word.

"TRAIL THOUGHT #7"

How are risk and discovery related? Can meaningful discoveries occur without a certain amount of risk?

8

DAVID'S ADVENTURES...COURAGE

THE DESERT OF Israel lends itself to alone time. The silent noth-ingness of sand and rock can calm a troubled soul and ease an anxious mind.

Because of its lack of water and good travel routes, the Judean wilderness and the Negev regions have been mostly uninhabited throughout history. The area is full of breathtaking views that are constantly changing. Mountains, cliffs, and chalk hills stand along-side plateaus, riverbeds, and deep canyons.

WILDERNESS SOLITUDE

David, of the Bible, spent a lot of time in the outdoors, sleeping under the stars, hunting and gathering food and water, building shelter, and perfecting his skills with a sling or other weapons. Like rocks in a tumbler, we too are shaped and refined by our experiences in nature. We are God's diamond in the rough.

Perhaps David picked up five smooth stones long before he faced Goliath. During his time alone with God on the hills around Bethlehem, I believe David acquired blessings of love, joy, peace, faithfulness, and goodness from the Spirit of God. These prepared him to face any battle by covering him with the full armor of God. These elements shaped his character, gave him courage, and concrete commitment to his heavenly Father.

David spent a lot of time alone with God on the hills around Bethlehem. He most likely prayed, communed with God, and wrote psalms, as he cared for his father's sheep. Alan Redpath says, "Perhaps David met with God one night under the stars as he saw the heavens declaring the glory of God. David's early life was marked by quietness."[1]

Solitude gives a man the opportunity to sharpen his skills and to sharpen his focus on God. Most great leaders know the value of escaping the noise of life to spend time alone. Courage and character are solidified on the mountain on God.

Solo time can be productive, but it's not meant to be all "me time," it should also be "God time." Up close encounters with God, in the wilderness, prepares us for up close encounters with the world. Charles Swindoll says, "It's in the little things and in the lonely places that we prove ourselves capable of the big things."

Places that seem lonely to some are safe zones to those seeking shelter from the storms of life. Hiking up the dusty ravines west of the Dead Sea, it's hard not to imagine David and his band of mighty men watching our every move from the caves and jagged hillsides that surround us.

My favorite stories in the Bible revolve around David, the shepherd boy from the outback, who became king. His was a life of adventure, action, and purpose. Men respond to great leaders who are tough but tender, who display courage and show compassion.

I picture David reclining next to a small campfire on a windswept hillside, his father's sheep silently grazing on new grass. At peace with himself and with God, he prepares a simple dinner, yet is always alert for bandits or wild animals, which could threaten the flock.

As David recalls the words of Isaiah 26:3 "You keep him in perfect peace whose mind is stayed on you," he begins to write, "The Lord is my shepherd, I shall not want. He makes me lie down in green pastures; He leads me beside still waters. He restores my soul."

From Abraham and Moses to David, John the Baptist and Jesus, all were strengthened by their experiences in the wilderness. The wilderness is a tool God used then, and is still using today to mold men.

The shepherd boy turned king, lived a life of action and adventure. David's life story includes some of the most exciting episodes found in the Bible. The stories of David defeating Goliath, his affair with Bathsheba, and his friendship with Jonathan, are all well know, often written about, and action-packed events in the life of David.

THE QUEST FOR ADVENTURE

As we continue our quest for adventure, I want us to draw inspiration from three lesser-known stories of David's life. These three events focus on courage, character, and commitment; the three stones of any discussion concerning David.

The land of Israel is filled with references to David. On King David Street in Jerusalem, we find the King David Hotel. Built in

1931, the hotel has played an important role in the history of Israel. It has been the site of frequent meetings of heads of state and is a national landmark.

The City of David is the birthplace of the city of Jerusalem, the place where King David established his kingdom, and where the history of the people of Israel was written. It is within walking distance from the Old City of Jerusalem and the Western Wall, and is one of the most interesting sites in Israel.

"In the year 1004 BCE, King David conquered the city from the Jebusites and established his capital there. It was here where the People of Israel were united under King David's rule, where the Ark of the Covenant was bought, and King Solomon built the First Temple."

Today the City of David is an archeological park that tells the story of the establishment of Jerusalem, its' wars and hardships, its' prophets and kings, and the history of the Jews during Biblical times.

The Tel Dan inscription, or "House of David" inscription, written on a ninth-century B.C. stone slab, was discovered in 1993 at the Tel Dan excavations in northern Israel. The slab of stone, or stela, proves that King David of the Bible was a genuine historical figure, and not simply the fantastic literary creation of later Biblical writers and editors.

Six clay seals found at the archaeological site in the northern Negev desert of Israel offer further evidence that supports the existence of the Biblical kings David and Solomon, says a team of archaeologists led by Doctor Jeff Blakely of the University of Wisconsin-Madison.

COURAGE OF DAVID

Courage is contagious, courage can be cultivated, and courage flows out of a concern over injustice. The term courage has become almost synonyms with King David. His exploits in battle have fortified men from soldiers to salesmen. David's adventures provide us with the needed ammunition to aspire to be men of action and courage.

David not only exhibited courage, he also inspired courage in his men. While on the run from Saul, men gravitated toward David because of his reputation as a man of courage. In his book "Stepping Up," author Dennis Rainey says, "Courage is contagious."

A discussion on courage makes me think of my friend Colonel Wes ReHorn, a retired Green Beret Commander. Just by standing beside him one can be inspired by his confidence, his courage is contagious. He was wounded in battle, led men into battle, and faced challenges that most of us only read about in books or see in the movies.

One of my favorite, lesser known, stories of David's adventures is found in I Samuel 26. If you remember, Saul had tried to kill David several times, but David gets out of Dodge and escapes to the Mountains. I believe he fled to the wilderness, not so much out of fear, as to avoid a confrontation with God's anointed king.

Ray Prichard describes it this way, "David and his men have been on the run, burning by day, freezing by night, climbing on the rocks like goats, fighting, running, hiding, always staying one step ahead of Saul." Picking the story up in I Samual 26:1-12, David and his men are hiding in an area of desolate wilderness in southern Judah. Saul is tipped off as to David's whereabouts and leads an army of 3,000 men to find David. (v 5) "Then David set out and went to the place where Saul had camped. He saw where Saul and Abner son of Ner, the commander of the army, had lain down. Saul was lying inside the camp, with the army encamped around him."

To quote Pritchard again, "This is like a scene from an old Western movie. At night, they would circle the wagons, put the women and children inside, with the men on guard outside. In this case, Saul's army is encamped in concentric circles with the king in the middle."

The adage "Find your enemy before he finds you," applies here. David finds Saul's camp before Saul finds him.

Ray Pritchard dramatizes the story this way, "It's Midnight, maybe a little past, when David pokes his head above the rocks. He is on the hill overlooking the camp. Ten thousand stars fill the desert sky.

Down below he can see Saul's army spread out before him: 3,000 men, their supplies, their donkeys, their wagons all carefully arranged. In the very middle of the sleeping bodies, he spots a spear stuck into the ground... Saul's spear. It was like a scepter, nearby was the king's water jug. Not a sound arises from the camp."

David issued a challenge to his men. He said, (v.6) "Who will go with me?" David was cultivating courage in his men, just as Jesus would when he said, "Come follow me." God is on the move. He is calling men everywhere to join Him in the great adventure.

David and Abishai, one of his mighty men, slip into Saul's encampment. The fact they could avoid detection is witness to their well-honed survival skills and their stealth.

Saul and his general Abner slept silently, at the mercy of David. Abishai whispers to David, "Today God has handed your enemy over to you. Let me thrust the spear through him into the ground just once. I won't have to strike him twice."

But David said to Abishai, "Don't destroy him, for who can lift a hand against the Lord's anointed and be blameless?" Instead, they took Saul's spear and water jug, "as an unmistakable sign to Saul that they had been there."

David yells, "Abner, O Abner. Wake up!" Abner replies, "Who are you and what do you want?" David replies, (v.15-16) "You're a man, aren't you? Who in Israel is your equal? So why didn't you protect your lord and king?"

In verse 18 we see that courage flows out of a concern over injustice. David asks Saul, "Why is my lord pursuing his servant, what have I done?" David's courage flowed out of his concern that Saul was not treating him fairly.

A true hero, David spared Saul's life once again. Alan Redpath, in his wonderful book, "The Making of a Man of God," considers what might have happened if David had let Abishai kill Saul.

"What would have been the effect on David's six hundred men? There are many evidences that the gentleness of David and his love for Saul influenced his men and showed up as part of their character in the days that lay ahead. If David had acted wrongly it would have affected his whole army and much of his godly influence would have been lost."

Adventurous courage is not just facing nine-foot tall giants with a handful of rocks, its showing mercy that honors God and sets an example for those who are watching you.

Modern day heroes like Pat Tillman and Jeff Streucker come to mind as I think of courage that wells up as a result of concern over injustice. After 9/11, Tillman gave up a lucrative NFL career with the Arizona Cardinals to join the Army. He was stationed and died in Iraq, fighting the injustice done to our nation. Captain Jeff Streucker was part of the rescue of the Black Hawk Down forces in Somalia in 1993. His heroic actions saved many live because God gave him courage over his concern for his fellow soldiers.

COURAGE FOR DAILY LIVING

While in Israel, I never once feared for my personal safety. Walking the streets of Jerusalem with my friends, I always felt at peace. We spent hours strolling through the Old City, visiting the many open-air markets and shops, and enjoying the fabulous food.

Most young Israeli's serve in their military. Both men and women are required to serve. Their desert tan and olive green uniforms are everywhere. Most carry Tavor, or Micro-Tavor Assault Rifles, as well as some type of handgun. Their service to their nation is a duty. Chesterton says, "Courage flows not from hate for those we face, but from love for those behind us."

The (IDF) Israel Defense Force also deploys The Iron Dome. This system is essential for protecting Israel from the smallest threats (rockets, artillery shells, mortars), which are targeted at civilians. It has successfully done its' job over the past few years, and remains the most combat-proven, modern air defense system in the world.

The Bible tells of God's love and protection of Israel. In Genesis 12:3 we read, "I will bless those who bless you, and him who dishonors you I will curse." One recent story tells of an Ultra-Orthodox high school teacher who claimed that a former student of his, who is the commander of an Iron Dome battery told him that the hand of God blew a Hamas rocket, that was aimed at the Azrieli Towers in Tel Aviv, into the sea. The Iron Dome failed to intercept the rocket three times.

In another story, a commander of the Givati Infantry Brigade described a mysterious fog that favorably covered him, and his troops, as they advanced on an enemy position in morning light, after their nighttime raid was postponed. The commander labeled the covering as clouds of glory.

Today, for those who make Israel their home, courage is required, just as it was in the time of David. Just as Abner and Saul were taken by surprise as they slept, today's Israeli's must remain vigilant if they are to survive as a nation.

CHARACTER OF DAVID

George Washington once said the character of a nation is determined by the character of its' people. The Jews of Israel are tough, emotionally hardened, and sometimes ruthless. Their image is epitomized in the "sabra," a cactus fruit, but also meaning a Jew born in Israel. In popular Israeli folklore, the Jews of Israel are "thorny and tough on the outside, but soft inside."

David's character, as a man and as a leader, can also be argued as being double-sided. There's no doubt David had flaws as a husband, a king, and a father, and many times he failed God.

But David's life was also characterized by his love for others, a generous spirit, his mercy, and his good heart. After all, David is the only person in the Bible to be referred to as a man after God's own heart. Adventure in life involves people. The friends, who go along with you, as well as those you meet along the trail, are important elements of any adventure.

Part of the character of Israel may be explained by the ever-present stresses of living in a predominantly military state. Common traits of this "national character" are arrogance, insolence (*chutzpah*), coldness, roughness, and rudeness.

"There is a coldness," notes Jewish scholar Norman Cantor, "a mystery, a distance from humanity about Israelis that anyone from another country who lives and works in Israel for a half a year will be impressed by, a deliberate and unadorned frankness, and lack of patience."

We all realize there are cultural differences, but the way we treat others tells a lot about our character. The following nugget illustrates the rock-solid, godly character of King David.

As you remember, Jonathan, Saul's' son, was David's best friend. Jonathan loved David and gave up his legal right to the throne to support his friend David.

In 2 Samuel 9 we find the story of Jonathan's crippled son Mephibosheth. After Saul and Jonathan had been killed, David became king. One of his first tasks as king was to seek out anyone remaining from Saul's family.

Mephibosheth, whose name means "mouth of shame," had been crippled at the age of five. Now age twenty, he was living with his nurse and her family in Lo-debar, a ghetto town located in Gilead. The name Lo-debar means "no hope, or no pasture" and is a desolate area northeast of the Dead Sea.

David's men find Mephibosheth and bring him to the king. Instead of killing him as Mephibosheth expects, David shows him grace and mercy.

In her blog, Brenda Parsons has a wonderful story entitled Living in and Leaving Your Lo-debar. "Little was he aware and did he know, the thing that would bring him out of hiding was grace, not harm. Absolute grace from the very thing that he had feared the most, the King's own hand. Instead of death, he had received a new life, in a way that he had not known since childhood. At last he would be able to sit at the King's table once again and enjoy the benefits of being an heir to a King. No more would he have to live in Lo-debar. King David even restored to Mephibosheth the land that belonged to his fathers. What a great picture of grace. David did for Mephibosheth what Mephibosheth could not do for himself. What a beautiful picture of what Christ has done for us."

Can we consider actions of grace to be exciting adventures? Maybe not in the normal sense of the term, but I believe our God certainly considers it an act of courageous manhood whenever we show grace and mercy.

We were not able to visit ancient Lo-debar but we did skirt the western side of the Golan Heights area, which is the general vicinity of Lo-debar. Traveling in our super-cool minivan, we crossed the barren countryside along Israeli Highway 99. Mike pointed out the area known as Nimrod's Castle on the hills to the east. Nimrod's Castle is a medieval Muslim castle situated on the southern slopes of Mount Hermon. It overlooks the Golan Heights and was built during the

Crusades to guard the major access routes to Damascus, Syria. I can only imagine the extreme physical commitment it must have taken to construct this massive rock fortress. The modern city of Nimrod is located nearby; it's the highest city in Israel, at 3,640 feet above sea level.

COMMITMENT OF DAVID

Adventure requires a commitment. Commitments of time, money and effort can't be underestimated. Preparing your mind and body for an expedition requires a strong commitment. Some describe commitment as courage being completed.

Below is a newspaper ad from 1908 seeking a commitment from men of adventure. It reads, "Men wanted for hazardous journey. Small wages; bitter cold; long months of complete darkness; constant danger; safe return doubtful; honor and recognition in case of success."

Sir Ernest Shackleton, a British explorer, placed the ad to recruit men for a daring expedition to Antarctica.

Commitment can be clearly seen in another of the lesser-known episodes of David's adventures. In 2 Samuel 23:13-17 we find David and thirty of his Mighty Men camped at the Cave of Adullum. Many believe this cave is near En Gedi, just west of the Dead Sea. Other scholars think the cave is near the Valley of Elah, where David defeated Goliath.

Three of David's men overheard him say, "If only someone would bring me water to drink, from the well at the city gate of Bethlehem."

These men were not told to go, just as they were not drafted to serve in David's army; they volunteered. Making their way some sixteen miles to Bethlehem required them to get past thousands of blood-thirsty Philistines who were camped in the Valley of Rephaim.

The three returned to the strong hold with water for their king. David is so overwhelmed by their commitment and courage he said,

"Lord, I would never do such a thing. Is this not the blood of men who risked their lives?" He refused to drink, instead poured it out as a sign of his commitment to these men and to God.

Mighty men of God live their lives with courage, character, and commitment. "God has room in his kingdom for many more mighty men. God is waiting for men to hear the call to the adventurous life of service to their King."

"TRAIL THOUGHT #8"

How are you cultivating courage in others? How are you growing in godly character? How are you moving from being interested in God to fully committed to God?

9

EXPEDITIONARY MEN...FREEDOM

WHILE HIKING THE Jesus Trail, I had time to remember and to thank God that I have been blessed to have many opportunities to visit amazing places. Salmon fishing on the Kenai River in Alaska, traveling the Amazon River on a refurbished banana boat, and exploring the Road to Hana on the Island of Maui, Hawaii, just to mention a few.

This big beautiful world that God has given us to enjoy is many times beyond description. Numerous times on this trip, I just sat silently amazed as I meditated on the beauty of our surroundings. I was so grateful. I felt unworthy of God's grace and the blessings of life, which many have not been able to experience.

Growing up in a poor family in the Ozarks, God enabled me to overcome many obstacles including poverty and personal rebellion. God has blessed my life with freedom in so many ways. Freedom from the consequences of sin and death are His greatest blessings.

As a child I dreamed of visiting exotic places I read about. I fantasized about having the freedom to explore. While reading Treasure Island and Robinson Crusoe, I pictured myself on a lush island picking fresh fruits and playing on the white sand beaches; something I have been able to experience on my numerous trips to the Islands of Hawaii.

While reading the old west novels of Louis Lamour, I fantasized about crossing the Rocky Mountains and camping under the stars in the high deserts of New Mexico. I have marveled at being able to experience both.

I began to see a pattern in the lives of men I met, many had something missing from their everyday lives. I began to realize that other men have similar dreams of adventure; the desire for freedom to roam. I recently asked several men why adventure was important to them.

WHY ADVENTURE MATTERS

Sargent Major Lance Nutt is the founder of Sheep Dogs Impact Assistance organization. Lance served 28 years as a United States Marine and has traveled to six continents.

Nutt said, "I find myself always looking over the horizon for the next big adventure. For me, adventure is important because it defines who I am, a man who loves to travel, loves to see beautiful places and meet interesting people."

Sheep Dog IA was founded to give retired or wounded vets, police officers, firemen, and EMT's ways to continue experiencing adventurous and purpose driven lives.

Lance goes on to say, "I find myself searching for something that will challenge my mind, body and soul. As a father of three young children, I am working hard to teach them the importance of challenging themselves through new and exciting adventures, whether through their imagination, during the travels we share, or through exploring new things...tastes, smells, and sights, all can be adventures in themselves."

Challenging men to get out of their comfort zone, to push themselves, and to serve others is at the heart of the mission of Sheep Dogs IA. Helping with disaster relief, participation in outdoor adventures, and helping the needy during Christmas and other holidays, offers the men and women of Sheep Dogs Impact Assistance unique opportunities for adventure. Nutt ended our conversation by saying, "Living life to its fullest is the key to truly enjoying the life that God has given us. We must not squander our freedom, or the beautiful gift of adventure."

Another man I spoke with said, "Adventure is the idea of heading out with a plan, but without really knowing what lies ahead, knowing that hard work and endurance is what it's going to take to make it through. That's freedom."

He smiled and said, "Just thinking about it gets my heart rate up and anxious to begin planning an adventure. Having an adventure is important because it helps push me to do better, and to push back against the status quo."

I asked him what prevented him from experiencing adventure, he pondered then replied, "There are lots of things keeping me from experiencing adventure: family, money, and self-doubt, but these are all just excuses."

He continued by saying, "The idea of adventures, like climbing Mt. Everest or hiking the Appalachian Trail, are so grand they sadly seem out of reach."

Colonel Wesley Rehorn is an amazing individual. His vast resume reads like a Jason Bourne or Jack Bauer movie. He has been in eighty-three countries across that world. He was wounded in battle and he has led men into battle. I recently asked him about leadership and adventure. "True leaders, men of action, men of conscience not only need adventure but should demand the opportunity. Our culture allows people to experience the world through so many mediums, television, movies, live streaming video on a home computer, on demand movies, You Tube, Face Book…the list is almost endless. But the understanding of how a man derives benefit from adventure is being lost to our present generation. There is no challenge, no risk, and no hardship associated with the electronic social media sources."

Rehorn continues, "One cannot adequately describe the pyramids, even after having seen an hour-long National Geographic documentary, without having actually visited the pyramids. The emotion, the heat, the size, and the setting …are all beyond words without having actually been to the location. "

Colonel Rehorn made another keen observation saying," One of our greatest treasures of man's struggles, trials and tribulations are recorded in books. As a society, we have given up the record of great men and adventure by ignoring books that we once read for the experience and the lessons learned from failure or success. Books that are written by men who have sought out challenge, weighed risk and danger, either taken or been thrust into leadership roles and have not only survived but excelled."

I could sense his passion for adventure as he continued, "I realize it's not possible for everyone to visit 83 countries, as I have been lucky enough to do. Nor is it feasible to have the opportunities to skydive, SCUBA dive, snorkel, ski, backpack and on one misguided attempt, snowboard, many of the greatest venues for adventure in the world. But everyone has the opportunity to read."

This question of why adventure is important gets men fired up and eager to tell you about the time they did this or that, or their trip to so and so.

Here are some other men's thoughts on adventure:

- *Brian:* "Life can become mundane; we can get in a rut where we are doing the same thing the same way the same day year in and year out. Adventure keeps men edgy, alert and aware of what is going on, it gives meaning to life by challenging men to reach heights that we may not even be aware that we are capable of in our everyday lives.

    I'm starved for adventure. I never do anything really risky or exciting. I told my wife, I know exactly what we will be doing six weeks from today, and it will be the same thing we are doing this week."

- *Bill:* "Besides being a distraction from our busy lives, adventure is our opportunity to test ourselves as men. Can we hunt and kill an animal, catch a fish, survive nature, all things that once defined a man. Today's world has made every attempt to emasculate men. We have an internal, genetic drive to be the provider/protector and we are being told that doing these things is wrong."

- *Danny:* Inside every man there is a boy who loves to explore. That is probably why I took my first sky diving excursion at age 65. It was a personal conquest, a bonding time with my oldest son, and a spiritual experience seeing the earth from what I envision could be the vantage point of angels!"

In researching this topic I found that men are starved for adventure. Men are hungry for healthy relationships with a small group of men they can experience adventure with. The obstacles to adventure I found include: a void of leadership, a perceived lack of freedom, financial limitations, daily responsibilities which suppress men's dreams, and a lack of developed dreams or plans all contributes to this frustration among men.

THE MAN OF ADVENTURE

An expedition is defined as a journey or voyage undertaken by a group of people with a purpose, usually that of exploration. Before the mission of an adventure is defined, there is a man who has a dream or a call to go. Something sparks a burning desire inside an individual, and then that spark is flamed into action.

For Moses, it was the burning bush. In the wilderness near Mount Horeb, an angel of the Lord appeared to Moses and called him to lead an expedition, an exodus to free God's people from captivity in Egypt.

For Abraham, it was a call to "go to the land I will show you." Through faith, he set out on a journey not knowing where he was going.

Author Loni Perry wrote in Top Ten Famous Explores and Expeditions,_"History is filled with brave explorers who tirelessly sought to fill out the edges of our known world. Often these expeditions have taken years of determined wandering into uncharted territory." Called, inspired, brave, tireless, determined are some ways these famous men and women of adventure are described.

All expeditions begin with a dream. Thomas Jefferson had a dream to expand the borders of the still young United States to the Pacific Ocean. This dream resulted in the mission to send Lewis and Clark to explore this newly acquired territory.

In 1914 Earnest Shackleton was determined to reach the South Pole of Antarctica. After months of preparation the mission was launched. During the voyage, Shackleton's ship *Endurance* was stuck in the polar ice, and he and his crew were forced to abandon ship. Due to Shackleton's optimistic leadership the crew was finally rescued after spending 497 days on the ice. In the book "Shackleton's Way," the authors refer to him as a Viking warrior with a mother's heart. Tough physically but also tender, Shackleton was bold in his plan, but cautious in its execution.

When God felt it was time to restore this broken world, he sent a man. His son Jesus "gave up the perks of paradise" to become a man, and save a broken world.

A MISSION OF ADVENTURE
In Jesus Christ, we have a man we can count on. God's mission is a great adventure that involves many, if not all twelve, of the "Elements of Adventure" discussed in this book. Mission revolves around the man Jesus. It's a worldwide movement in which all of us can play a part.

When I talk to men who hunger for adventure, I sometimes hear the need to be involved in a mission. Many are men who have accomplished amazing things in their business or civic organization, but still feel underutilized.

Expeditionary men go. Moses goes to the Promised Land, Paul goes to the gentiles, and Nehemiah goes to rebuild the walls. Lewis and Clark go to explore the American west, Shackleton goes to the ends of the earth, and Jesus goes to the cross.

Thankfully, in our spiritual expedition we have the Bible as our map. A guidebook, we can count on for direction, comfort, and wisdom. In chapter eleven I will expand more on the map.

EXPEDITION WITH FRIENDS
Going on an adventure with a small group of men is much different than traveling with your family. There is normally less talk among men, definitely fewer bathroom stops, less concern for comfort, and more emphasis on staying on schedule.

On the Jesus Trail trip to Israel, we slept in tiny bunks in crowded hostels, on the ground in tents, or in hammocks. We didn't have regular showers or regular meal times. Many times, we were content with our own thoughts, and rarely made small talk.

Patrick Woodhead warns, "Tiny idiosyncrasies, such as snoring, chewing too loudly, or fidgeting in the tent, can be a source of incredible tension that builds up over the days of confinement." My four friends were extremely patient with my slower pace of hiking and exhibited a biblical longsuffering with my super loud snoring. I won't mention their corny jokes, poor driving or limited navigation skills.

I certainly enjoyed my time in Israel with Christian brothers, but was also happy to be home. Author Josh Gates says, "Travel does not exist without home.... If we never return to the place we started, we would just be wandering, lost. Home is a reflecting surface, a place to measure our growth and enrich us after being infused with the outside world."

Pure adventure with other believers allows us to be infused with the awesome beauty in the world.

IMPACTFUL EXPEDITIONS

Expeditions are about impacting the world. Men want to leave a legacy, to explore for fortune or fame, or be the first to accomplish a dangerous feat. Whatever the motive, the mission is to make an impact.

The Corps of Discovery, directed by Lewis and Clark, had a far-reaching impact on our nation. Increased knowledge of our geography and topography of the west, hundreds of new plants and wildlife species identified, the rise of the fur trade and the negative impact for the Plains Indians way of life.

Without a doubt, the most important expedition of all time was when Jesus came to earth to rescue a sinful people. His mission was spelled out before time began; His plan was to carry out the will of the Father.

Galatians 1:4 says, "He gave Himself for our sins to rescue us from this present evil age, according to the will of our God and Father." That is the mission that matters.

It starts with a dream of going to distant lands and then others catch a vision for the mission, and a map is developed. The map for an expedition is not always complete at the start of the journey.

With God, the Bible is a proven road map, written to tell us the epic story of Jesus. From creation to the second coming, in its pages we find wisdom, direction, comfort, and a way to know Jesus as our personal savior.

My friend Dave Schell says, "Having a quest gives me a sense of purpose and builds self-esteem, as I prepare mentally and physically to tackle an adventure."

Dave goes on to say, "Adventure gives an escape from day-to-day pressures and reality of life. My most priceless adventure has been father and son time. No price tag can be put on that time together."

Adventure brings people together. The shared struggles and the satisfaction of completing the journey, creates a lifetime impactful memories.

Another friend shared a cool story about a hike their family went on to "Hemmed in Hollow" along the Buffalo National River in northwest Arkansas. This section of the Ozarks is beautiful but extremely rugged. The trail out of the hollow rises about 1,500 feet and is just over three miles in length.

During the intense climb up the steep bluffs, his kids thought they wouldn't make it. They struggled and complained all the way, but they did it! Now whenever their family is in a tough situation they say, "at least it's not as tough as Hemmed in Hollow!"

Another friend Caleb Gordon says, "God created us with a desire for adventure; as men, it's what we long for. I personally believe when you're in the midst of God's adventure for your own life, that's when you are truly satisfied. We mess up when we begin to chase after other forms of adventures."

Randy Sauer, a friend and men's leader in Joplin, Missouri says, "Adventure allows me to satisfy my desire for manhood from another dimension that I don't experience in an office job. For young men, I believe the more avenues they can experience to feel a sense of accomplishment, the better. It builds confidence."

For me, special places like the Leatherwoods, Calico Rock, Panther Mountain, and Big Sugar Creek, all bring back happy memories of past adventures. Hunting the Leatherwoods with my son, fishing the White River at Calico Rock, camping and deer hunting around Panther Mountain, and boot camps along Big Sugar Creek, are all places God used to grow my faith.

12 ELEMENTS OF SPIRITUAL EXPEDITIONS
I have identified twelve elements of my own personal and spiritual expedition experiences, I hope they will help you grow in your faith.

1. You should be able to write your personal journey, your testimony of what Christ has done for you, and share it with others.
2. Be prepared to share stories of people who have helped you on your expedition. Give Bible examples, plus people in your life.
3. Identify obstacles you overcame, plus force multipliers, which have energized and propelled you on.
4. Share discoveries you have made along the way, discoveries about yourself, about human nature, and about God.
5. How has God sustained you on your journey? Given strength, comfort, peace, and protection.
6. Why is your journey important to others; family, friends, co-workers? It's important because your story is part of the epic story of God's redemption.

7. Why do we share these stories of our expedition? It's that the world may know that our God is a big God who is involved in the lives of ordinary men like you and me.

8. Be prepared to use your message to encourage men to join a corps of discovery, to be a part of a band of brothers that can change the world for Christ.

9. What are the consequences of failing to join the **expedition,** the dangers of staying where it's safe, comfortable, easy, where we are always in control on the situation?

10. What are the short-term and eternal rewards of joining and completing your God given expedition?

11. How can we miss discoveries along the way, covering a lot of territory but never finding the truth of God's Word?

12. What drives you on? What pushes men to strike out?

As you think deeply about these twelve elements of a personal and spiritual journey it will force you to better know what you believe, and hopefully you will come to know God better.

Josh Gates reminds us, "Adventure rewrites the routine of our lives and wakes us sharply from the comforts of the familiar. It allows us to see how vast the expanse of our experience. Our ability to grow is no longer linear but becomes unrestricted to any direction we wish to run."

Adventure may involve times of heart-pumping stress, black diamond slopes, and class four streams, the "uncharted rivers and lands where the wild country comes alive," but it may also come in the quiet, pools and prairies of solitude and reflection.

It's difficult to recapture the sense of time, or realize the magnitude of the Bible stories, unless you hike the paths, stroll the narrow streets, and experience the tastes and smells of the area.

As I think back of my time along the Jesus Trail and the other places we visited, I'm amazed at how the experiences of being there makes the Bible come alive. To follow the narrow streets of the old city of Jerusalem is an urban adventure. It's one of the oldest cities in the world, and every square inch has been fought over, burned, rebuilt, and worshiped by the followers of three world religions. To walk the Via Dolorosa, "The Way of the Cross" in old Jerusalem and see the fourteen Stations of the Cross along the way is a moving experience. To stand on the Mount of Olives looking out over the city is almost like an act of praise and worship. As Dale and I discuss the Eastern Gate, or Golden Gate, of the Old City, someone begins to recite the prophecy found in Ezekiel concerning the gate.

PATHFINDERS

On Day 9 we continue our tour of Jerusalem. Our steps took us to the flat-top of a building to get an unobstructed view of the Temple Mount, a holy site of Islam. The temple and its' Dome of the Rock are sad reminders that not all paths lead to Jesus.

Paths don't just appear out of thin air. All paths begin with a pathfinder. Trails have a trailblazer, someone who has bravely gone before us to prepare the way. A pathfinder is defined as a person who finds or makes a way, a route, especially through a previously unexplored or untraveled wilderness. It could also be a scout who goes ahead of a group and finds the best way to travel through an unknown area

Sacagawea was a pathfinder. She was a Shoshone Indian woman who served as an interpreter and guided Lewis and Clark across the rugged Bitterroot Mountains in 1805. Her wilderness wisdom most likely saved the expedition from certain death.

John Wesley Powell was a pathfinder, a trailblazer. During the Civil War, Powell lost an arm at the battle of Shiloh. After the war in 1869, he organized the first successful attempt to run the rapids of the Colorado River through the Grand Canyon.

Another well-known pathfinder and trailblazer in American history includes Daniel Boone, who blazed the Wilderness Road, a famous path through the Cumberland Gap of Kentucky into the heartland of America.

One of the best-known trailblazers in the Bible was John the Baptist, born to parents Zacharias and Elizabeth, who lived in the hill country of Judea. Luke 1:80 says, "And the child grew and became strong in spirit and he lived in the wilderness until he appeared publicly to Israel."

Wearing a camel hair shirt secured with a leather belt, his diet consisted of locusts and wild honey. Yum Yum! This guy was the original mountain man. John's mission can be summed up by one word, "preparer." A pathfinder goes before, makes a way, for those who are to come. John preached about the coming kingdom and the need to repent. He prepared the way for the coming of Jesus.

As born again Christians, our trailblazer is the Way-Maker, Jesus. His death on the cross has prepared a way for us to live eternally with God in heaven.

Expeditionary men are found in every generation, striking out to explore new lands and unchartered seas. They are men who are driven to see what's over the next mountain and who as David Foster says, "Are unafraid of unrutted roads, muddy trails, and unfamiliar territory."

"TRAIL THOUGHT #9
"Why is adventure important to you? What is keeping you from being involved in outdoor adventure?

10

ACT LIKE MEN...VIGILANCE

"**B**ACK UP, BACK up," Bill warns as Mike turns our van onto a dead-end street in a congested Arab neighborhood near Mount Carmel. Not a safe place to be this time of day, we quickly reverse direction and make our way out of the village.

It was getting late in the day and we were trying to locate a place to camp for the night. At the time, I thought Mike and Bill were over-reacting, but later as I came to understand the many possible dangers I was thankful to have two well- trained, and hyper-vigilant men leading our expedition.

Today's men are under attack...all you have to do is watch any TV commercial or sitcom and see how men are portrayed as stupid, weak and lazy. We seem to have lost the glue of common sense that once held our nation together.

Garrison Keillor wrote of this in "The Book of Guys," "Men are in trouble these days. Years ago, manhood was an opportunity for achievement, and now it's just a problem to be overcome."

Rugged Faith Ministries was founded from a deep-concern over the feminization of today's men, and a heart-felt passion to restore a biblical world-view that values masculinity, family stability, and common values.

Darrin Patrick warns about a crisis of manhood in America in his book, "The Dude's Guide to Manhood," he calls it a "guide filled with wisdom and practical knowledge that charts a course back to manliness."

Patrick speaks about how manliness is about character and not personality. He asserted, "A real man can be tough and tender." Patrick claims "most men didn't have real men to guide them to be the men they were created to be."

Ten years ago, when I retired from teaching and coaching in the public schools and founded Rugged Faith Ministries, I was beginning to see this unhealthy trend. I'm not suggesting that all boys and men must be rugged outdoorsmen to be masculine, but I have experienced and have seen the positive benefits of placing men in the classroom of the outdoors.

YOUNG MEN NEED ADVENTURE

In her blog, Candice Gaukel Andrews says, "Adventure experiences remedy a societal ill: loss of adventurous children and the extinguishing of wanderlust. Today, the United States is facing what some have described as an epidemic: the loss of the adventurous childhood. The Outdoor Foundation reports that youth participation in outside activities has declined for three straight years. And when parents overschedule kids and insist on being involved in every one of their activities — when they become "helicopter parents" — they kill a child's desire to explore. The spark for wanderlust goes out, permanently."

Christian adventure is especially effective with youth. Tim Hansel, in his book "Holy Sweat," puts it this way; "Young people need large doses of adventure to change, discover, and grow. If they aren't sufficiently challenged by real-life adventure, they will seek and find fictitious adventures of significantly less value."

To quote David Murrow "Boys are kinetic creatures. Young men need to move. During their teens, boy's bodies are awash with testosterone. It makes them aggressive, risk taking, and fidgety. Healthy outdoor activity is one of the keys to unlocking a young man's heart."

Rugged Faith Ministries has had several opportunities to partner with Teen Challenge Adventure Ranch, which is in northwest Arkansas. Hopefully our involvement with Teen Challenge has helped cultivate masculinity in their students.

Teen Challenge Describes itself as an "Adventure-Based Therapeutic Boarding School for Troubled Boys." The Teen Challenge program is designed to help boys when:

- Their behavior is out of control
- Counseling and other outpatient treatments aren't working
- Their problems are persistent or even worsening despite promises to change
- Inappropriate behaviors are placing his (or your) health or life at risk
- They are involved in illegal activities or drugs

- They were expelled from school or are facing legal problems
- They are deeply entangled with friends who are a negative influence
- They keep returning to negative behaviors, even after periods of time when they had been doing well

Adventure is an effective tool God uses to teach men to be men, because the journey from boy to man can be a challenging adventure. As Church leaders, parents and businessmen, we must be ever vigilant for ways to get our youth involved in the outdoors.

Dennis Rainey, of Family Life Today, has developed another tool for men, it's a study entitled "Stepping Up." This study explores the three stages of a man's life. Stage one is Boyhood, stage two is Adolescence, and stage three is Manhood.[1] Each phase of life has its challenges, but the adolescence stage seems to be the most difficult for males.

On the tenth day of our trip, while we were standing in line to enter the Western Wall, or Wailing Wall in Jerusalem, we heard music and singing behind us. It was a ceremony known as bar mitzvah. A Jewish boy automatically becomes a bar mitzvah upon reaching the age of 13. This ceremony recognizes the time a boy becomes a man.

Bar mitzvah is not about being a full adult in every sense of the word, ready to marry, go out on your own, earn a living and raise children. The Talmud makes it perfectly clear that while thirteen is the proper age for fulfillment of the Commandments, eighteen is the proper age for marriage and twenty is the proper age for earning a livelihood.

Here in America, we don't have a predetermined time when boys move into manhood. Thus, we find an often unhealthy, extended adolescence that allows young men to retain their childish ways into the later teens or even early and mid-twenties.

Pastor James McDonald says, "What society and church so desperately need are men who embrace all that God created them to be, who long to follow God without limits and meet the needs of those around them without hesitation."

Eric Mason, in his book "Manhood Restored," agrees. "Men are so unclear about who they are supposed to be, because we, in the church, have failed to give them a true picture of the ultimate man Jesus Christ. Jesus alone has exemplified manhood. If we want to be conformed to His image, most especially as men, we need to understand this example more deeply."

A FOUR-PART CHALLENGE

Every year our team develops a four-part message for our Rugged Faith Boot Camps. In 2015 we chose the theme of Act Like Men, taken from I. Corinthians 16:13.

About two thousand years ago, the Apostle Paul gave four short imperatives to the church at Corinth. Paul admonished them to, "Be watchful, stand firm in the faith, act like men, and be strong."

Adventure requires varying degrees of these same four elements. To remain safe as we explore the outdoors, hiking, fishing, rock climbing, hunting, kayaking, or whatever your favorite adventure might be, we must be watchful, stand firm, act like men, and be strong.

Again, this is not an attempt to "spiritualize" adventure, but to make us more aware of the benefits of adventure in every area of our lives, including physical, mental, and spiritual.

I want to compare the critical need to remain spiritually watchful and the necessity to be vigilant, physically and mentally, as you enjoy outdoor adventure.

BE WATCHFUL

The first of these admonitions from Paul is to be watchful. Paul was warning the people of Corinth to watch out for both false teachers who attempt to deceive them and watch out for division among themselves.

Some Bible translations say be on guard, be alert, or be vigilant, all issue this warning to Christians. This is what I call the "*3-D Warning*" of the Days, the Devil, and Duty. The days in which we live are evil, the Devil is our enemy, and it's our Duty as believers to be vigilant.

We live in perilous <u>Days:</u> terrorism, political correctness, and racial division all present varying degrees of danger. As Christians, we must be watchful because of the days in which we live. Paul reminds us in 2 Thessalonians 3:2, "We live among perverse and evil men." Not everyone is a Believer. Because of the days in which we live, we are in the world, but not of the world and we must be watchful.

In 1 Chronicles 12:32 we read about the Men of Issachar. They are described as "men who understood the times…" This should be our model as godly men. Common sense comes from common values and we must be alert, understanding the days in which we live.

We must also be watchful because we have a powerful and ruthless enemy who is out to destroy us. 1 Peter 5:8 warns us to "Be watchful, your adversary the <u>Devil</u> prowls around like a roaring lion looking for who he can devour."

The final 3-D warning is duty. It's your <u>Duty,</u> as a man, to protect and provide for your families. Vigilance is critical as we endeavor to lead at home, at work and at church. In Deuteronomy 11:16 we are warned to, "Take heed of yourself, that your heart is not deceived." We have a duty to be on guard.

We don't have to deal with bloodthirsty Philistines as David did, or encounter hostile Indians as Lewis and Clark did. However, our adventure, exploration and expeditions all require vigilance. Physical danger can be around every bend in the trail. From wild animals and poisonous snakes, to wild rivers and streams, the outdoors presents us with challenges that require vigilance.

Adventure requires that we watch out, watch in, and watch up. Yes, we enjoy the jaw-dropping scenery the outdoors offers, but we must always be alert to possible danger out there. We must also be watchful of our hearts and minds to avoid sinful behavior as we watch for Jesus' return.

BE A MINE SWEEPER

My dad was in WWII and saw action in some of the most intense, bloodiest battles of the war in the Pacific. The battles were fought on numerous island scattered across the region. Some of the most valuable assets the USA had during these island battles were its mine-sweepers. These ships had the important mission of clearing floating mines from sea-lanes around the islands. The *USS Vigilance* was one such ship. It was commissioned in 1943 and saw almost constant action the final two years of the war.

The minesweepers duties included the following six elements of vigilance.

1. Locate and remove dangerous mines
2. Shield ships from incoming Kamikaze attacks
3. Guard the entrance to the homeports
4. Watch and listen for possible danger
5. Put out fires caused by enemy attacks
6. Rescue and care for the injured

To be a godly man requires vigilance much like a minesweeper. Ask yourself the following questions;

1. Am I locating and removing danger that could harm my family?
2. Am I being a shield to protect my family, others, and myself from Satan's attacks?
3. Am I guarding the entrance to my home, filtering out any destructive content from TV, Internet, and dysfunctional visitors?
4. Am I watching and listening to my children and my wife to protect them and to show them respect?
5. Am I ready to put out fires whenever problems arise?
6. Am I equipped to rescue and care for family members who are experiencing hurts and pains?

STAND FIRM

Rock walls and rock fortresses dot the countryside along the Jesus Trail and in other parts of Israel, at Mount Arbel, and nearby Horns of Hattin, and at Masada near the Dead Sea

Perhaps the best known is the Western Wall in Jerusalem. It is the most holy place accessible to the Jewish people because of Muslim control of the Temple Mount. Known in recent centuries as the "Wailing Wall," this section of the wall was built by Herod the Great as a retaining wall of the Temple Mount complex.[2] Standing firm for centuries the Western Wall is a remnant of the Second Temple destroyed by Rome in 70 A.D.

Paul's second admonition to the church at Corinth was to "Stand firm in the faith." Paul challenged the Corinthians to resist the tug of culture and the tide of false teachers who were intent on toppling the early church.

We face many of the same currents as the church at Corinth faced. Subtle forces that infiltrate the church with the goal of planting doubt and disrupting unity.

Built in 1867, the Ar Men lighthouse off the northwest coast of France is known as "The Rock." It is one of the best-known lighthouses in the world because of it isolated location, its considerable difficulties in construction, and the now famous video of the lighthouse standing firm against the intense waves that are common in that area. The wind and the waves pound the Rock, but it stands firm.

Nature can throw some awesome force at us. My hometown of Calico Rock, Arkansas has seen some floods of near biblical proportion in the past twenty years. In March and April of 2008 the White River was a monster. It came roaring out of the hills of north Arkansas, spurred on by near twenty inches of rainfall over a five-day period. As huge trees, debris, and even homes were uprooted and sent crashing into it, the old Highway 5 bridge at Calico Rock stood firm.

Like a bridge over turbulent water and a lighthouse in the storm, it's reassuring that our faith is built upon the Rock. Jesus Christ is our firm foundation, enabling us to stand against the storms that life hurls at us.

HOW MEN ARE TO ACT

Paul's third challenge to the Corinthians is to act like men. James McDonald has the best explanation of this I have ever heard. McDonald reminds us in his book, "Act like Men," that men were created in the image of God and as such we, "Don't act like a woman, don't act like a child, and don't act like an animal." These three common sense statements are at the heart of what it means to be a man.

Gender confusion is the term used today to describe the myth that God made a mistake when he created male and female. Godly men don't act like a woman. God created the two sexes to complement one another, each with its own purpose and role.

My friend Brian Center tells a story that wonderfully illustrates the problems that occur when men act like children. Brian says, "As a manager of a retail outlet I had a thirty-seven-year-old male employee who was constantly late every Monday. When I asked him to explain why he was late only on Mondays," he replied, "I'm a gamer. I play video games with people all over the world. I sometimes play thirty-six hours straight on week-ends."

Center asks him about his family and explained the problems he was causing by being constantly late. "If you are late one more Monday I will be forced to fire you." Come Monday, guess what? Yep, the guy came dragging in late again. Did you let him go I ask? "Of course, I fired him, I couldn't let his childish behavior negatively affect the business."

Christian men don't act like animals. Animals are selfish. Godly men are selfless. Brian relates another story of his dog Zeke. "Whenever I come home my dog Zeke comes bounding around the corner to meet me. He knows that he is about to get something to eat. But, if a friend is with me and the friend had a big juicy steak, who do you think Zeke would run to, me or the guy with the steak?" This story illustrates the fact that animals are selfish; they are loyal to who-ever feeds them. As Christian men, we should not act like an animal. We should be selfless, not selfish.

In his weekly blog, Pastor Todd Wagner of Watermark Community Church in Dallas, Texas lists 5 Characteristics of a Godly Man. The five fit perfectly with the theme of "Act Like Men."

1. Step Up, men must initiate and lead. Be a man of action. Hate apathy and reject passivity.
2. Speak Out: Silence during sin is a sin. Be courageous. Fear God not man. Speak the truth in love.
3. Stand Strong: Don't give in when you are challenged, at-tacked or criticized.

4. Stay Humble: Be vigilant against pride. Get the log out of your eye. Don't think less of yourself, but think of yourself less.

5. Serve the King: Seek first His Kingdom, His glory, and His righteousness. Hope in the eternal. Live for a greater reward.

BE STRONG

Part four of Paul's message to the church of Corinth is to be strong. Sounds simple enough, right? Go to the gym, lift some weights and be strong? I think Paul's idea involved being strong in your faith. A strong faith means a dependence upon God. When we try to be strong in the flesh, we become prideful and cause problems.

Many strong, athletic men, who love the outdoors, are the ones who are most likely to be killed or injured in extreme adventure. Some take foolish risks, they stretch the boundaries of sound judgment, and they ignore good advice.

Remember Samson, the strongest man in the Bible? He had so much potential wasted because of pride and rebellion. Pastor Mark Atteberry, in his book, "The Samson Syndrome," lists the Twelve Tendencies of Strong Men.

1. Strong Men Tend to Disregard Boundaries
2. Strong Men Tend to Struggle with Lust.
3. Strong Men Tend to Ignore Good Advice
4. Strong Men Tend to Break Rules.
5. Strong Men Tend to Overestimate Their Own Cleverness.
6. Strong Men Tend to Use Anger as a Tool of Control
7. Strong Men Tend to Repeat the Same Mistakes
8. Strong Men Tend to Have Large Egos
9. Strong Men Tend to Take Foolish Risks

10. Strong Men Tend to Struggle with Intimacy
11. Strong Men Tend to Take Too much for Granted
12. Strong Men Tend to Lose Sight of the Big Picture

God is a God of adventure; pushing, pulling, and coaxing us toward our full potential. He has a special plan for your life. He wants you to prosper in your spiritual life; he wants you to fulfill your mission, he wants to give wisdom to those who seek it.

While a loss of common sense is most likely due to the loss of biblical values that once bound our nation together, another reason for the lack of wisdom may be the death of the middle class in America. Today we are seeing the middle class being squeezed. Loss of jobs, stagnant wages, higher taxes, and fewer new businesses being started has led to the shrinking of the middle class. While the rich get richer, many once considered middle class are joining the ranks of the poor.

Aristotle once said, "He who greatly excels in beauty, strength, birth, or wealth, and he, on the other hand, who is very poor, or very weak, or very disgraced, find it difficult to follow rational principles."

If we are to regain our common sense Godly men must be watchful, stand firm in the faith, act like men, and be strong.

"TRAIL THOUGHT #10"
How has the meaning of what it means to act like a man changed?

11

THE MAP...DIRECTION

THE JESUS TRAIL is a trek that takes some planning. Some of the trail winds through towns and villages on paved streets and is not always well marked. However, using a hand-help GPS unit and maps printed off Google Earth, we stayed on course most of the time.

GPS, or Global Positioning System, was developed for surveying and navigation purposes. The GPS system has three categories of data; waypoints, routes, and tracks.

Waypoints mark the coordinates of a location, a route is a collection of waypoints linked by a straight line, and a track is a detailed record of a trail displaying curves on the path.

Blaze colors painted on rocks, curbs, and trees mark the Jesus Trail. White/orange/white stripes are normally visible and right angle markers indicate turns.

There are other trails in Israel, including the Israel National Trail, which stretches the length of the country from Lebanon in the north to Egypt in the south. This rugged trail is 620 miles long, and is on my bucket list of to do adventures. This trail's markers can sometimes cause confusion to hikers who are following the Jesus Trail.

In his book, "Points Unknown" author David Roberts says, "GPS and sat phones have transformed exploration, some say they have emasculated adventure." The hiker on the Appalachian, or Pacific Crest trails that is exhausted, or soaked in a downpour can whip out his sat phone and call his mom to come get him.

Roberts adds, "Some old explorers thought adventure was always a mistake. Adventure only happened when you screwed up. Many feel adventure has been corrupted by packaged tours, which blur the boundaries between tourism and adventure."

MAPS
Maps have always fascinated me. As a child, I would draw maps of our neighborhood, maps to some secret hideout or tree house, and maps of make-believe battlefields or cattle drives. Today I'm still interested in maps, although I'm not one of those "Mapifiers' as John Steinbeck called them "whose joy is to lavish more attention on the sheets of colored paper than on the colored land rolling by." I collect historical and interesting maps. My favorite maps are the historical maps of the Lewis and Clark Trail, the Pony Express

Route, Santa Fe Trail, treasure maps, vintage topo maps, and other adventure maps.

Topo, or Topographical maps, the green ones, are very popular with explorers, hunters, and backpackers. These maps show elevation of the land, contours, shapes, plus natural and manmade landmarks. You can purchase the paper version on get them on your I-phone or loaded onto your Garmin unit.

Men love maps and many men seem to have a built-in, God-given sense of direction. I have spent hours in the woods and wilderness over the past fifty years, and I can't ever remember being physical lost. God has blessed me with a good sense of time and direction.

A map is a plan. It shows details of the trail or river ahead. Like a guidebook, it can point us in the right direction. Pastor Rick Warren says, "Your abilities are the map to God's will for your life. It points the direction. When you know what you're good at, then you can know what God wants you to do with your life."

Lost

Lost is a terrible place to be, with no sense of direction, confused, and anxious. Being lost in the wilderness can be life threatening. Why do people get lost? It could be they didn't plan their journey; they misread the signs and trail markers, or it might be darkness or weather related.

Whenever we misread the signs or miss the route markers we are in danger of being lost. As a young man, I was more interested in dollar signs than God's signs. I was more interested in the markers on the ladder to success than the biblical markers of significance. I'm thankful now for the guidance of a God that loves me.

Without a life-map, we are lost. From Genesis to Revelation, border to border, the Bible is the epic story of God's great adventure.

Without the Bible as our guide we can't know our purpose, our abilities are wasted, and we wander in darkness.

God has a plan for your life. In Jeremiah 29:11 we read, "For I know the plans I have for you," declares the LORD, plans to prosper you and not to harm you, plans to give you hope and a future."

Darkness and storms contribute to men being lost. We live in a world of sin and darkness. Satan is the great deceiver, in 2 Corinthians we read, "The god of this age has blinded the minds of unbelievers, so that they cannot see the light of the gospel that displays the glory of Christ, who is the image of God."

Beth Moore says, "Satan has his champions of darkness who use deception and despair to discourage men and try to keep them down."

I once worked as a tour guide at Blanchard Springs Caverns during the summer months. The U.S. Forest Service has developed lighted paths through this natural underground cathedral that attracts thousands of visitors each year.

As a tour guide, I had several opportunities to allow our guest to experience total darkness. After guests were safely seated, I would turn off all the lights. Everyone was surprised at the complete absence of light; total darkness is really dark. You can understand how darkness can contribute to someone being lost. Occasionally a guest would have a lighted wristwatch or phone. This tiny amount of light seemed like a spot light when you are in total darkness.

In much the same way, as Christians our light shines brightest when times are the darkest. Your life is a light to those lost in darkness. Part of God's great adventure is equipping you to rescue those who are spiritually lost.

DIRECTION
Direction and distance are key factors in wilderness navigation. Being keenly aware or your surroundings, knowing how to read a compass

or a GPS, and the ability to properly judge distance are all critical during an adventure.

I still like a paper map because it does not require batteries or a signal to power it up, but new technology has replaced the need for maps and scouts who went ahead of the group to blaze the trail, search for watering holes, and finding the best route through the mountains.

Great explorers of the past used the sun and the stars as reference points to guide them. Physical landmarks, like Devil's Tower and Great Falls, guided the Corps of Discovery and those who traveled the Oregon Trail.

Finding the right direction in life is perhaps just as important as the right direction on the trail. "You are only as good as the map you use." God's word offers the believer a detailed instruction book to guide your life.

The Bible has over seventy-five references to God directing our path, or making a way for those who will follow. In Isaiah 43:18 we read, "Look, I am about to do something new... I will make a way in the wilderness, rivers in the desert."

My wife and I have a small real estate investment fund we call For-Ward Partners, LLC. The name indicates that the fund is for Jack and Brenda Ward. Of course, the hope is that the fund is also advancing in value, moving forward.

In life, we have several options as far as direction and distance are involved. You can move right, left, forward, backward, downward, or upward.

I believe your direction in life will affect your impact on others, and your distance from God can determine your decision-making ability.

Forward is the road to success; we must keep moving forward if we are to complete the expedition and mature in your faith. In Psalm 4:25 we read "Let your eyes look forward; fix your gaze straight ahead." Forward direction is characterized by persistence, faithfulness, and a commitment to finishing strong. Moving forward requires risk. Like snow skiing down the slopes, if you lean back you will fall, but if you lean in, press forward, you can better control your speed and your direction.

To go backward in your adventure or in life can be costly. Hiking through the city of Nazareth, the trail was not well marked. This resulted in several instances of backtracking, until we found the proper exit out of the old city.

Going backward in your faith is what some call drifting. Nobody drifts toward God. Because of our sinful nature, we are naturally inclined to drift away from God. Pastor Wes George in a recent message entitled Extraordinary Grace said, "If we are trending backward it's because of our ignorance of Scripture, influences which are negative, or immaturity in our faith."

Early in our marriage, Brenda and I, along with some friends, were camped at Norfork Lake in north central Arkansas. After a fun day on the water, we tied the boat to some rocks and turned in for the night. When morning arrived, we came out to find that the boat had come untied and had drifted about a hundred yards into the lake. Much in the same way, we tend to drift away from God if we are not securely anchored in the faith.

Jeremiah 7:24 warns "But they did not listen or pay attention; instead, they followed the stubborn inclinations of their evil hearts. They went backward and not forward."

Working in ministry to men for the past ten years I have seen numerous men go into a downward spiral due to use of drugs or alcohol, metal depression, and family breakups. God wants to direct our lives. Upward is the way to victory. When we turn our eye to Jesus He breaks the downward spiral, he rescues the wayward son or daughter, and he put us back on the path to peace. He is the benchmark from which everything else is measured.

A benchmark is a topographic symbol, often a simple metal disc, set in stone and inscribed with a triangle and a small mark in the center. Whether in the wilderness or in the city, a benchmark is a known point, a permanent point of reference, which can help us better understand exactly where we are, almost anywhere in the world.

In his book, "A Godward Life" John Piper confirms our need for a savior who guides us. The books focus is on the radical difference it makes when we choose to live with God at the center of all that we do.

Several outdoor organizations offer excellent programs to help people find direction in their lives. *Outward Bound* is the leading provider of experiential and outdoor programs for youth and adults.

What sets Outward Bound apart from many of the other organizations that provide wilderness expeditions and training is that we bring an equally high level of emphasis and performance to teaching to the outcomes of character, leadership and service.

Another is *Way Forward Adventures*; their guides will lead your group on an adventure that will result in life transformation, self-discovery and stories to tell for years to come. Their slogan is "Adventure+ Discovery=Impact."

Direction is important to a follower of Christ. As we submit to his leadership he will show us the way. Proverbs says, "In all your ways acknowledge him, and he will direct your paths."

If you were on the wrong trail, what would you do as soon as you discovered it? You would turn around and go back to a recognizable point where you got sidetracked.

Charles Swindoll in his book on King David says, "God re-routed David's life." We too must sometimes reroute our lives whenever we see we are going the wrong direction.

DISTANCE & SIZE

Whenever we read about Israel, or hear of it in the news, we often fail to consider its size. It's only eighty-five miles across the nation of Israel at its widest point, and its only 290 miles long at its longest point.

Israel's distance and size, in comparison to it impact on the world, is shocking. Constantly in the news, this tiny nation is at the center of the world geographically, and politically.

Distance can be deceptive when looking out across the barren Judean Wilderness of Israel, I recall asking one of the guys on our trip how far it was across the Dead Sea to the nation of Jordan? The answer surprised me because the dense haze made it appeared much further.

Distance from God determines so much in our lives and the Bible has a lot to say about this. In James 4:8 "Draw near to me and I will draw near to you." In Psalm 145:18 it says, "The Lord is near to all who call upon Him."

Someone said that distance is relative; it all depends on where you are, compared to where you are going. It's 238,900 miles to the moon, so how far is it to heaven? The answer, my friend Rusty Jones says, is eighteen inches, from your head to your heart, the longest expedition some men will ever attempt.

On a recent hike of the Jesus Trail, Dennis Lewon, of Backpacker Magazine asks, "I wonder what it was like to hike for miles on a trail much like this with only thin sandals on your feet?"

It's hard to imagine hiking the forty miles barefoot or wearing only the thin leather sandals of Jesus day. I was blessed as my Merrill hiking shoes and Smart-Wool socks protected my feet well after getting past the first day shock of steep hills on paved roads.

To cover the entire forty miles of the Jesus Trail normally takes three to five days. Compare this to the 2,168-mile long Appalachian Trail, which normally takes between five to seven months and only about twenty percent of those who start to go the distance.

Time spent on the adventure trail gives you opportunities to think deeply. You can map out your life, ponder mistakes you have made, consider what you should contribute to others, and dream of how you can impact the world for good. Walking gives you time to immerse yourself in the culture, time to observe the people, landscape, and time to listen.

FOLLOW ME!

In Matthew 4:13 we discover the foundation of what has come to be known as of the Jesus Trail. "Leaving Nazareth, he went and lived in Capernaum by the sea." Jesus leaves his boyhood home of Nazareth and walks the forty miles east to Capernaum on the Sea of Galilee.

In his Backpacker Magazine article, Lewon wonders "if this was just another trek for him or did Jesus pause on the ridge overlooking Nazareth to say a final sad goodbye to the people who rejected him?"

In her book, "Walking in the Dust of the Rabbi Jesus," author Lois Tverberg offers some wonderful insight into the life and times of Jesus and what it means to imitate him in our walk of faith. Tverberg reminds us that to be a disciple of Jesus requires us to know why and how he lived, so we can follow him more closely.

Her book makes the Holy Land come alive as she describes the "silvery green olive trees on the Galilean hills, feel the rocky path under your feet, and smell the dust as you follow the Rabbi Jesus."

Tverberg wants us to grasp the importance of distance as we walk so close to Jesus we are covered with the dust from his sandals.

BOUNDARIES, BORDERS, AND LIMITS

Since a physical Jesus is not with us today, we need a map. That map is the Bible. A recent blog post Ron Hurtgen says, "The Bible is a road map. It tells us more about ourselves, the problem of human condition and joy than we could ever imagine. If you'll open a Bible, you'll be surprised where it takes you.

Maps displays borders, boundaries, and limits. In a land where every square inch of dirt is claimed, sacred, and fought over, boundaries can mean life or death.

The Bible describes the boundaries of the Garden of Eden in Genesis. In Exodus, we find the boundaries of the Promised Land. The dimensions of Solomon's splendid temple can be found in I. Chronicles 29:1-19, and even the size of Heaven can be found in Revelation 21:15.

God is a God of minute detail; distance and time are part of his creation. Boundaries and specifications are important to the one who created them.

Roads were built for a reason; boundaries and borders marked for a reason. A boundary is a line that denotes or defines where one person's space ends and another's begins.

God gives us boundaries for our own good and sometimes we establish boundaries that keep God at a distance or in a compartment. Lifeway's Barney Self says, "Biblically speaking, boundaries are related to self-control. Boundaries can be used in healthy ways and sinful ways. The way to know which boundaries are godly is to examine the motive."

Boundaries, borders, limits were all God's idea. I have found that selfishness is a problem in my life. I see it in my life, and I see it in the lives of most men I meet. Dying to self is hard. We cling to our rights, our stuff, and our pet sins.

I want to mature in my walk with Jesus to the point where I can say, "there are no boundaries between us." My space ends and I am annexed into His kingdom. What's mine was never really mine in the first place. Borders are erased and I constantly live in His promised land. I want to be on "uncharted rivers of grace where the wild country comes alive." I want to take others on this "Upstream adventure' to the source of the Living Water.

The prayer of Jabez is found in 1. Chronicles 4:10. "Jabez called upon God to expand his boundaries, or enlarge his borders." For many of us who love the outdoors, adventure is an answer to this ancient prayer. As we explore new lands God opens our eyes to new and wonderful possibilities. As we surrender our agenda He expands our ministry.

I know I'm a nerd, but maps are cool. They get me excited about my next adventure. I can trace the route, plan the stops, and dream of what I will see and do. I encourage you to M.A.P. your life; Make A Plan. God invested a lot in creation. He designed it for you to enjoy. Get your boots on, get out there, go!

"TRAIL THOUGHT #11"

What would you do if you were lost in the wilderness? What would you do if you knew your family members or best friends were eternally lost, living without Jesus?

12

NEXT STEPS...CHALLENGE

A s we reached the end of our Jesus Trail adventure, I felt both sadness and fulfillment; Sad the trip had ended yet fulfilled by the amazing experiences and close friendships I had developed.

In this final chapter, I want to remind you that Christian adventure should be designed to lead people closer to Christ and challenge you to grow in your Christian walk. Adventure is more than filling empty days at tourist sites or at the beach. Its' purpose is to find God in the great outdoors. The reward of the route is a closer relationship with the Father.

Spilling across parts of four Arab nations is the legendary sea of sand known as The Empty Quarter. Covering some 225,000 square miles of harsh, mostly-uninhabited desert. It's one of the hottest and driest environments on earth. The challenge of crossing this vast wasteland was first accomplished by the British explorer Bertram Thomas in 1930.

The Empty Quarter correctly describes the life of many men who thirst for adventure. Are you parched for adventure? If so, you are not alone. In my interviews with dozens of men I found the following responses, men described their need for adventure in the following ways; Hungry, starved, thirsty, crave, absence of passion, something missing, the need to explore, restlessness.

In his classic work, "Travels with Charlie," John Steinbeck reminds us "Adventure pushes us to abandon the sweet trap of comfort and safety and embrace the uncomfortable and the unknown." A divine restlessness is not unhealthy. God planted that feeling within a man to push him to reach his God-given potential.

If you are not a Christian, God can fill this restless void in your life. In 1. Peter 1:18 he says, "God paid a ransom to save you from the empty life you have inherited." The major aspect of that ransom of course is our salvation, but another is creation. He died to reclaim his creation for us to enjoy. In Roman 8:19 we find, "For the creation waits with eager longing for the revealing of the sons of God."

In his blog called Great Big Scary World, Jamie Bowlby-Whiting says, "Many men say they have never had a truly great adventure. Many say I do not know what an adventure is, but I want to experience more of the world and that is an adventure in itself. I wish to observe the world like I have never seen it before. I want to takes notes, collect memories, and focus on everything."

In a recent article by Candice Andrews entitled "Ten Reasons Why Adventure is Good for You," she makes the point "Adventure travel feeds your dreams and builds your confidence. But no matter how many steps it takes to get there, the one thing that's certain about adventure to spectacular nature spots is that it soon becomes addictive."

Andrews goes on to say, "Experiencing one wilderness just doesn't seem to be enough; your soul quickly calls for more. And each time you go, you find yourself changing. Adventures build your confidence; and with each successive one, you challenge yourself just a little bit more."

The editor of National Geographic Travel Magazine once suggested that the Cycle of Travel went like this: 1.Dream 2.Plan 3.Go 4.Share. In your efforts to squeeze an element of adventure into your busy life; I suggest that you use this cycle as a starting point. First dream. Dream big. Allow yourself to dream of an adventure you would like to experience in the next year. Begin to pray about it, discuss it with your family, share your vision with others and ask them to pray that God will bless you with the finances and the time to accomplish this dream.

Second, plan your adventure. Even before you have secured the finances or carved out the time, it's okay to begin planning the details and start the needed training. Third, go. Just do it. Make it happen; maybe it's only a day trip or a weekend, put your boots on and go. Finally, share your experiences with others. Tell how God provided the finances and the time, share the challenges and the memories with those you love, and give God the glory. I want to challenge you with the following Code of Adventure.

THE RUGGED FAITH CODE OF ADVENTURE

1. Infect others with the adventure bug by sharing your stories.
2. Infuse the gospel into all your adventures, share about Jesus.
3. Include your family in your adventure, sharing the memories.

   Sharing the excitement of your past adventures has value to your family and friends. Just as courage is contagious, true adventure can be infectious. To infuse the gospel into your adventures can be as simple as sharing the love of Jesus with those you encounter along the trail, in the airport, and at the car rental place. To include your family in your adventures begins with sharing your dream to go, including them in the planning, and whenever possible, involve them in the challenge.

A challenge is a call to take part in something that may seem unattainable. The challenge may come from someone inviting you, or the challenge may come as you invite others. A challenge is somewhere between an ultimatum and a dare.

Matthew Robinson says, "I believe we were created to conquer the challenges this world laid before us. Genesis 1:28 confirms this, "God blessed them; and God said to them, "Be fruitful and multiply, and fill the earth, and subdue it.""

Robinson reminds us, "We are constantly finding ways of conquering/subduing the ever-changing world around us, some with pure motives and others with not-so pure motives. Much of our innate characteristics is birthed within us from creation and is only understood through our relationship with the Creator. Every challenge we face serves to bring us to a greater revelation of who He is and who we were created to be."

As I look back on my days in Israel I'm forever thankful that my friends challenged me to be a part of this adventure. It was one of the most meaningful experiences of my life.

THE NEW WILDERNESS

It may seem that all the good stuff has already been done. Some feel there is nothing felt to explore, and wilderness is no longer with us. To quote Martin Holland, "A friend of mine said to me recently that there is nowhere left to explore. It made me sad that he felt that way, but kind of motivated at the same time because I knew with absolute certainty that he was utterly wrong, and that humanity's journey of discovery is just warming up."

If you are one who asks what's left to explore, let's begin with outer space. "To boldly go where no man has gone before." Space travels anyone? How about the oceans? Water covers about three-fourths of the surface of the earth. How about the underworld of caves? Add to these the many packaged travel tours, and the new world of (VR) Virtual Reality and we have endless opportunities for adventure and exploration in the future.

Two of my personal favorites for future adventure include, exploring the mystery of God, and the search for truth. In Isaiah 58:8 He has "For my thoughts are not your thoughts, and your ways are not My ways." This passage challenges me to explore the deep mysteries of God, to strive to know Him better.

In Colossians 2:2-3 we see, "My purpose is that they may be encouraged in heart and united in love, so that they may have the full riches of complete understanding, in order that they may know the mystery of God, namely, Christ, in whom are hidden all the treasures of wisdom and knowledge."

Possibilities of hidden treasures of wisdom and knowledge are the lure of adventure to a follower of Christ. "There is no understanding of God apart from a personal relationship with His Son Jesus Christ. The key to having the full riches of complete understanding is to be born again by the divine power of the Holy Spirit."

Adventurers are seekers. Always searching for another new horizon, a hidden mountain lake, or the next class-4 whitewater. As Christians, we should be seekers of truth. Let's unpack that thought. The Greek word for truth is *aletheia*, which literally means to "un-hide" or "hiding nothing." It conveys the thought that truth is always there, always open and available for all to see, with nothing being hidden or obscured.

Biblical truth is under attack in our culture. Many today are not impressed with what the Bible says on a subject. Anyone claiming to have absolute truth in matters of faith and religion is considered to be "narrow minded." Andy Stanley points out, "Many aren't exactly on a truth quest. They're on a happiness quest."

With the Bible, we will never run out of areas to explore. The following passages offer an incredible adventure into the nature of God worthy of our study.

SCRIPTURE ON GOD'S GREAT OUTDOORS

- GENESIS 1: 1 In the beginning God created the heavens and the earth.
- PSALM 19:1 The heavens declare the glory of God; the skies proclaim the work of His hands.
- PSALM 95:4-5 In His hands are the depths of the earth, and the mountain peaks belong to Him. The sea is His, for He made it, and His hands formed the dry land.

- PSALM 102:25 In the beginning you laid the foundations of the earth, and the heavens are the work of your hands.
- ISAIAH 55:12 ......the mountains and hills will burst into song before you, and all the trees of the field will clap their hands.

    ROMANS 1:20...Since the creation of the world God's invisible qualities–his eternal power and divine nature–have been clearly seen, being understood from what has been made, so that men are without excuse.

ADVANCE

As Rugged Faith Ministries enters its second decade we have thoughtfully considered the next steps for this ministry. With prayer and God's blessing, I envision Rugged Faith advancing. Advancing the gospel, advancing our reach and advancing our impact.

Through a strong partnership with Rowdy Mott of Bear Hollow Ranch, and a dedicated group of volunteers and financial supports, I see no reason this ministry can't fulfill its mission and glorify God for years to come.

Future plans call for annual "Pure Adventure" trips, which offer men opportunities for exciting adventure outings. Our 2017 schedule of trips include hiking a section of The Ozark Highland Trail in northwest Arkansas, ATV Adventure along the Lolo Trail in Montana, and another 10-day trip to Israel to hike the Jesus Trail.

Rugged Faith Boot Camp will remain the anchor events of our ministry, offering weekend retreats for men and boys. Camps will continue to offer the same blend of outdoor adventure and sound biblical teaching. Our mission remains the same; we call it "GPS" (Guide, Prepare, Support.) Guide men to a deeper understanding of Jesus Christ, Prepare men to be godly leaders, and Support the local church.

My personal ministry will hopefully include more writing and speaking on issues important to men. With God's grace and guidance, I dream of mission trips to Brazil and China, to teach men about courage, character, and commitment.

My quest for adventure, God willing, will begin to pick up momentum as I have more time. Planning the next five years, my bucket list, or "Next Step Adventures" as I prefer to call it includes;

1. Hike the St. Paul Trail in Turkey
2. Raft the Colorado River through the Grand Canyon
3. Explore the Alaska Highway across Canada to Fairbanks
4. Hike the Israel Trail north to south across Israel.
5. ATV the 245 mile Paiute Trail in Utah.

Next Step is an effort to get men my age and older involved in adventure. The Baby-Boom generation is a huge segment of our population and many of these men have the time, the finances, and the desire to experience adventure after years in the workforce.

Next Step Adventures will not only offer the boomers opportunities for adventure, but also opportunities to get involved in local service projects, and in foreign missions.

The Next Step "3-P's of Adventure" includes; Plan to be flexible, Pace yourself, and Pack light. Any adventure includes the unexpected. The key to success, enjoyment, and safety is to always be flexible, be willing to change your plans on the fly.

I have learned that hard way that I must also pace myself. In wanting to experience as much as possible in the limited time on the trip, I learned early on that I must pace myself to accomplish the fullest. I encourage you to pack light to avoid problems in airline travel, and packing light frees you to pick up and go at a minute's notice.

Next steps for many men who retire revolve around daily golf and playing cards at the country club. For others, it's fishing and more fishing. Still others take up woodworking, reading or another hobby. There's nothing wrong with any of these when done in moderation, but God never intended men to retire from Kingdom work.

Experts say men are more susceptible to depression in retirement, in part because their identity is more closely tied to their careers compared to women. "For a lot of men, it really is a loss of a sense of identity – something that we get from work," said clinical psychologist Marnin Heisel, director of research and associate professor in the department of psychiatry at the University of Western Ontario in London, Ont.

While employed, men develop a strong routine and many of their friendships come from work, says Dr. Heisel. "For a lot of guys, when they retire, they lose that social network and social connection and the meaningful contribution they get out of what they do."

"It's not the job or the money that men miss so much in retirement, but the socialization and self-esteem that work brings," says Ken LeClair, co-chairman of the Canadian Coalition on Seniors.

As they travel the world to soak up experiences, too many seniors inevitably lose track of what really matters, their connections to family, friends and community.

LeClair says, "There's a way out of this trap. Retirees should think about using all the advantages that make a bucket list possible, such as wealth and vigor, to build something much deeper and more meaningful. Instead of taking a dream vacation to chase fleeting thrills, they should use their time to create something more lasting. Such as building bonds with family, getting involved in church service projects, and going on short-term mission trips."

Rugged Faith will continue to partner with other ministries to reach people for Christ. Our prayer is to extend the ongoing relationship with Teen Challenge Ranch of Northwest Arkansas to include other Teen Challenge facilities across the region and the nation. We have seen God do amazing things in the lives of these young men as they experience God in the outdoors.

Rugged Faith plans to continue to develop Godly leaders who love the outdoors and use creations as our classroom.

In his book "River Reflections," Verne Huser expands on the need for wilderness. "The wilderness is a special place for transforming leaders. Throughout history, God has used the wilderness as a special place for transformation. The Biblical text indicates that God's strategy for developing mission-focused young leaders has often involved transforming wilderness experiences. This is an integral part of God's design for apprenticeship. Yet today in our increasingly urbanized world young people are less able to experience the wilderness."

The challenges most all non-profit ministries face are financial sustainability and volunteerism. Rugged Faith has been blessed in both areas. While finances are never enough to fully-fund everything we would like to accomplish, God has blessed us with generous individuals and churches that support our work. Our team of volunteers has been amazing. For the past ten years, I have had the honor of serving with some wonderful men who came along side me to help carry out the mission of Rugged Faith.

I want to challenge you to consider the next steps you need to take to become a fully committed follower of Jesus Christ. I know that many of you are committed and are living out the calling God has placed on your life. Other may be in the very common situation of being interested in God, but still holding onto categories of life that aren't full surrendered to God.

As you come to the end of this book, turn back to the Table of Contents and re-read the twelve elements of adventure, one for each chapter. Prayerfully consider each of the twelve elements and ask God to point out areas where you need to grow. Maybe it's perseverance, or courage, or godly character. It's my prayer that God will call you to the amazing adventure that comes with a full commitment to follow Him. God is on the move. He is challenging you to "Come follow Me." He's asking, "Who will go with me?" The adventure has a purpose, the time is urgent, and God is building a mighty army of committed men. A joy-filled life awaits any who will accept the challenge.

"TRAIL THOUGHT #12"
List some items on your bucket list of adventures. Consider a spiritual adventure that would stretch your limits of comfort.

ENDNOTES

CHAPTER-1

"Men Need Adventure: How the Christian Adventure Differs from the World's"
Dr. Jared Staudt, www.ThoseCatholicMen.com 01/08/2016

Gallantoro; The Return of the Gentleman, August 25, 2015
"Men and Their Need for Adventure" www.gallantoto.com

"Hiking the Jesus Trail" Anna Dimtaman & David Landis, 1st Edition April 2010
Village to Village Press, Harleysville, PA

"What is Adventure and Why do you Need it as a Man," Derek Loudermilk
The Good Men Project, August 8, 2015

"Every Man Needs Adventure" Chris Hutcheson, www.artofmanliness.com 12/2008

CHAPTER-2

"What is Adventure and why do you need it as a Man," Derek Loudermilk
The Good Men Project, August 8, 2015
www.goodmenproject.com

Solid Rock Outdoor Ministry, Laramie, WY 2016

"The Odyssey Expedition," Graham Hughes, 2013

Why Men Need to Teach Boys Perseverance, Rick Johnson "The Making of a Man" Revell Publishing, June 1, 2013

"Who is the Greatest Adventurer of all Time," Men's Journal, Editors, 2014
www.mensjournal.com,

'Hiking the Jesus Trail," Anna Dintaman & David Landis
Village-to-Village Press, 1st edition, April 2010
www.4thmusketeer.org

CHAPTER-3
"The Possibilian" Burkhard Bilger, The New Yorker, April 25, 2010
http://www.bibleplaces.com/mtcarmel/

New International Version Bible, Zondervan Publishing, NY, NY 2015

"How the Ancient Israelites Got Their Water," Tony Benson, The Testimony Magazine March, 2006

http://www.bibleplaces.com/engedi/

Arkansas Parks & Tourism, TV AD 2016

"Why Men's Ministry Needs Outdoor Adventure" Outdoor Leadership, March 2015, Doug Self, The Orchard Church

"Expeditionary Man" Rich Wagner, Zondervan Publishers, 2008

"Why Men's Ministry Needs Outdoor Adventure" Doug Self, The Orchard Outdoor Leadership, March 2015

Campus Crusade for Christ, CRU 201

CHAPTER-4
"Esau Rising" Bill Cloud, 2016, WND Books, Washington, DC

"The State of Church Planting in the United States" Ed Stetzer & Warren Bird

"The Road Headed West" Leon McCarron, 2014, Summersdale Publishers NY, NY

"Jesus Never told us to Plant Churches." Trinity Jordan, Influence Resources, 2012

P. J. Weeks, Raindown Ministries, Laurel, MS, 2014

"Hiking Through" Paul Stutzman, Revell Publishers, 2012

"Man on the Run," Zeke Pipher, Howard Publishing, 2012

"The Importance of the Dead Sea Scrolls." Author, Will Varner, Associates for Biblical Research Copyright © 1997

"How Women Help Men Find God" David Murrow, Thomas Nelson, 2008

Chapter-5
https://en.wikipedia.org/wiki/Masada

"Jewish History" Joseph Telushkin, William Morrow and Company, NY 199
"March to Glory, Soldiers Hike to Receive Berets"

Wilderness Ministry Institute, Fort Collins, CO, Web page 2016

"The Apostle: The Life of Paul" John Pollock, David C. Cook Publishing, 2011

His Water International, www.hiswater.org Bangor, Maine 2015

"The Lonely Land" Siguar F. Olson, University of Minnesota Press, 1961

"Joe Hardcore," Erik Hedegaard, Men's Journal, June 2014

"Extreme Sports, What's the Appeal?" Heather Hatfield, WebMD, 2006

"Risk; Better to Lose your life than to Waste it" John Piper, Crossway Books, 2013

"5 Important Reasons to Embrace a Little Adventure" Lindsay Holmes, Huffington Post, October 8, 2014

"That the World May Know" Ray Vander Laan, web site, 2015

"The World's Unlikeliest Trail" Brian Mockenhaupt, Backpacker Magazine, September 6, 2016

"5 Reasons Active Family Travel is Growing" Loren Siekman, Pure Adventure 2015

CHAPTER-6
"Crossing our Jordan" Lloyd Stilley, Pastor First Baptist Church, Jasper, Alabama. 2015

"What Does the Bible say about Consecration?" www.gotquestions. org 2016

CHAPTER-7
"Corps of Discovery" U.S. Army Center of Military History, May 2015

"The Journals of Lewis and Clark" Meriwether Lewis, William Clark,

"Undaunted Courage" Stephen Ambrose, Harper Collins, 1997

"Walking the Bible" Bruce Feiler, Harper Collins, 2001

"13 Things Mentally Strong People Don't Do" Amy Morin Harper Collins, NY, NY, 2014

"Caesarea Maritima" www.BiblePlaces.com

"Paul's Missionary Journey Through Perga and Pisidian Antioch" Noah Wiener www.biblicalarchaeology.org May 16, 2016

CHAPTER-8

"The Judean Desert" Go Israel, 2015, www.goisrael.com

"The Making of a Man of God" Alan Redpath, Revell Publishers, 1962

"David, A Man of Passion and Destiny" Charles Swindoll, Thomas Nelson, 1997

"City of David" Israel Land of Creation, Staff, www.goisrael.com

"Tel Dan Inscription" Biblical Archaeology Society, Dec 8, 2015

"New Finding Suggest Biblical Kings David and Solomon Actually Existed" James Hardin, 2104 Near Eastern Archaeology

"The Case of the Missing Spear" Ray Pritchard, Keep Believing Ministries, October 15, 2000

"The Message" Eugene H. Petersen, 2002

"Top 10 Most Powerful Weapons of the Israeli Military" NRP, Defense Encyclopedia, January 30, 2015

"Rumors Abound But God's Protection of Israel is no Fable" Raphael Poch

Breaking News Israel, August 11, 2014

"Jewish Character Traits in Israel" Jewish Tribal Review, Editor 2015

Jewish Tribal Review, Norman Cantor, 2015

"Living in and Leaving Your Lo-debar" Brenda Parsons, Higher Ground Devotionals, March 2013

Steven J. Cole, pastor of Flagstaff Christian Fellowship, Flagstaff, Arizona. Bible.org Sept 10, 2013

CHAPTER-9
"Top 10 Famous Explorers and Expeditions" Loni Perry, January 8, 2010
www.toptenz.com

"Shackleton's Way" Morrell & Capparell, Penguin Books, August 2002

Patrick Woodhead, UK Telegraph, January 2015

"Destination Truth: Memoirs of a Monster Hunter". Josh Gates Gallery Books, October 11, 2011

"The Lonely Land" Sigurd F. Olson, From A Collection of River Writings,

University of Minnesota Press, March 12, 1961

"Who was John the Baptist?" Wayne Jackson, Christian Courier, Sept 25, 2016

CHAPTER-10
"The Dude's Guide to Manhood," Darrin Patrick, Thomas Nelson, January 2014

"Stepping Up," Dennis Rainey, Family Life Publishing, 2011

"Bar Mitzvah" Tracey R. Rich, Judaism 101, 1996

"Act like Men," James McDonald, Moody Publishing Oct 1, 2014

"5 Characteristics of a Godly Man" Todd Wagner, Watermark Community Church Blog, August 21, 2013
""The Samson Syndrome" Mark Atteberry, Thomas Nelson, 2014

CHAPTER-11
"Hiking the Jesus Trail" Anna Dintaman and David Landis, Village to Village Press, April 2010

"Points Unknown" David Roberts, Mariah Media, 2000

"Unbranded" Ben Master, Video Documentary, Texas A&M Press, 2106

"A Godward Life" John Piper, Multnomah Press, October 5, 2001

Outward Bound, www.outwardbound.org Golden, Colorado, 2016

Way Forward Adventures, Richardson, TX, 2016

"The Jesus Trail; Hiking From Nazareth to the Sea of Galilee" Dennis Lewon, Backpacker Magazine, March 2012

"Walking in the Dust of the Rabbi Jesus" Lois Tverberg, Zondervan, 2013

"The Bible is a Road Map for Our Lives" Ron Hurtgen, SE Missouri News Blog, May 20, 2012

CHAPTER-12
"Ten Reasons Why Adventure is Good for You" Candice Gaukel Andrews, Good Nature Travel Blog, July 7, 2015

"The Treasure of God" www.gotquestions.org

"Men Vulnerable to Boredom, Depression in Retirement" Brenda Bouw
The Globe and Mail News, November 26, 2015

"It's Time to Rethink the Bucket-List Retirement" Marc Argonin, Wall Street Journal, March 20, 2016

"River Reflections; A Collection of River Writings," Verne Huser, Editor
Globe Pequot Press, Chester, CT 1985

APPENDIX A

EQUIPMENT LIST...JACK WARD
MOST ITEMS PURCHASED AT LEWIS & CLARK
OUTFITTERS AND
PACK RAT OUTDOOR SUPPLY

Backpack...Gregory Z-40...3 lbs, 5 oz
Water Bottle...REI 32 oz
Sleeping Pad...Therma-Rest Neo-lite...1 lb 3 oz
Tent ...Big Agnus ....2.5 lbs
Sleeping bag...Marmot Hydrogen 1 lb 8 oz
Pillow...Therma-Rest (small) .07 oz
Jet Boil mini stove...1 lb
Fuel for Jet Boil...3.55 oz
2-pants...Columbia convertible
2-shirts...long sleeve... Columbia & Mtn Hardware
1-jacket...Northface Venture- hooded
2-long underwear top & bottom...Under Armor
3-undershirts...Exofficio
3-underwear....Exofficio
4-socks...Omni Wool & Smart Wool
Hiking Sandals...Teva...1 lb 4oz
Hiking Shoes...Keen
Gloves...
Sunglasses
Cooking gear...plate, bowl, spoon, fork, cup, scraper/brush
Coffee Filter...
Food...see attached list
Notepad Water-proof & Pencil

Olympus VN-8100PC ...mini digital recorder with lapel mic
I-Phone
Call Pod Duo...phone battery pack
Neck Wallet...passport, DL, cash, Visa card,
Personal Hygiene Items...see attached list
Towel...2 MSR
Extra batteries, AA & AAA
Sock Cap
Sun Cap/hat
Bible -pocket size
Headlight...Black Diamond
Mini Mag Light
Small fanny Pack/day trips
Waterproof Matches
Swim Suit
Flip-Flops (Cheap)
2-Bandana's

PERSONAL ITEMS

Toilet Paper
Body Wipes...8 pack Fresh Bath
Mini Wipes/Soap...Sea to Summit
Hand Sanitizer
Tooth Brush/Tooth Paste
First-Aid items; band-aids, blister care, bandage, Badger foot balm, etc
RX items + OTC items
Small camp mirror
Sun Screen
Clothesline (Para cord) 3 clothes pins

Razor & Bar Soap
Deodorant
Toothpicks
Earplugs
Large freezer bags for washing clothes
Laundry soap

FOOD

6- Instant Oatmeal Packets
8-Sugar Packets… 1oz ea
1-Dried Cranberries, Raisins, Peaches…6 oz ea
1-Almonds, Walnuts, Pecans…4 oz ea
Coffee…6 Instant packets..Starbucks Via
Coffee…6 oz Ground/brew
Coffee Mate…16 mini packets
6-Hot Cocoa mix…Starbucks 1.25 oz eac
1-Beef Jerky 6 oz bag
1-Trail-Mix 8 oz bag
6-Power Bars assorted brands
8-Peanut Butter…1.5oz packets
6-Candy Bars…Payday, Snickers
2-Wild Salmon…Seabear 3.5 oz packets
4-Tuna…Star-Kist… 3.0 oz packets
1-Crackers 24 pack
8-Gatorade Drink mix…1.2 oz packets…Lemon Lime, Orange
6- MRE's…Beef Stew, Potato/Cheddar Soup, Brisket Entrée, Chili &
Macaroni, Beef Ravioli, Chicken & Rice…8 oz each
Salt & Pepper
Catsup & hot sauce packets

APPENDIX B

OUTDOOR ADVENTURE MINISTRIES

Christian Adventure
Peterson Outdoor Ministries
Blind Faith
Cave Time Ministries
Xtreme Outdoor Ministries
Solid Rock Outdoor Ministries
Majestic Outdoors
Ironman Outdoors
God's Great Outdoors
Campfire Cowboy Ministries
Heart of the Outdoors
Texas Baptist Men Outdoors
The Call Outdoor Ministries
Rain Down Ministries
Jason Cruise Outdoors
Outdoor Truth Ministries
Take it Outside Ministries
Wilderness Ministry
High Country Ministries
Rugged Faith Ministries

Christian Waterfowlers Association
Benchmark Ministries
Spring Valley Ranch
The 4th Musketeers
Summit Outdoor Ministries
Focus Outdoor Ministries
Legacy Outdoors Ministries
Christian Sportsman
FCA Outdoors
True North Outdoors with Dad
Deer Boy Outfitters
Lifelines CRU
Kids Outdoor Zone
Final Descent Ministries
Spiritual Outdoor Adventures
Outreach Outdoors
Triumph Outdoors
Fathers in the Field
Christian Bow Hunters of America

APPENDIX C
25 Book's That IMPACT Men

1. Wild at Heart…. By John Eldredge
2. Why Men Hate Going to Church…By David Murrow
3. What God Does When Men Lead…By Bill Peel
4. Unleashing Courageous Faith…By Paul Coughlin
5. Disciplines of a Godly Man…By R. Kent Hughes
6. Scared Marriage…By Gary Thomas
7. The Hard Corps…By Dai Hankey
8. Twelve Ordinary Men…By John MacArthur
9. Expeditionary Man…By Rich Wagner
10. The Making of a Man…By Alan Redpath
11. Man on the Run…By Zeke Pipher
12. Battle Ready…By Steve Farrar
13. Sun Stand Still…By Steven Furtick
14. Accept no Mediocre Life…By David Foster
14. Eternal Security…By Charles Stanley
15. Man in the Mirror…By Patrick Morley
16. A Guide to Biblical Manhood…By Randy Stinson
17. Transforming Grace…By Jerry Bridges
18. Sleeping Giant…By Kenny Luck

19. The Purpose Driven Life…By Rick Warren
20. You Were Born for This…By Bruce Wilkinson
21 The Measure of a Man…By Gene Getz
22. Act Like Men…By James MacDonald
23. What Makes a Man…by Bill McCartney
24. Stepping Up…By Dennis Rainey
25. Kingdom Man…By Tony Evans

APPENDIX D

"Rugged Faith Sportsman's Fellowship"...*Sportsmen's Clinics 2015*

April 9...Stephan Richardson, World Champion Turkey Caller

April 16...Rogers Cravens, JT'S Crappie Fishing Guide (Fishing)

April 23... Brian Johnson, Ozark Sportsman Supply (Archery)

April 30... Allen Treadwell, Bass Pro Shops (Shotguns)

May 7...Jim Potts, Lewis & Clark Outfitters (Camping)

May 14...Buck Ortega, Planet Fitness,

May 21...Steve Dunlap, Arkansas Game & Fish Commission

May 28...Tim Sallee, Christian Waterfowlers Association

June 4...Ethan Korpella, Boy Scouts of NWA, Dutch-Oven Cooking

June 11...Wes Sharp, UFC Gym, Mixed Martial Arts

June 18...Jim Zalenski, Rugged Faith Ministries, Hiking the Ozarks

June 25...Russ Taylor, Beaver Lake Bass, Striper Fishing Guide

July 2...Mike Tarvin, Chaplin Tyson Foods (God & Country)

July 9... Mark Clippinger, Supt. at Hobbs State Park

July 16...Hunter Henry, Cody Hollister, Razorback Football

July 23...Matt Tate, Integrated Survival Systems (Survival Training)

July 30... Rick Rainwater, GPP Cycling (Mountain Biking)

August 6...Jake Reynolds, Transformation Taxidermy

August 13...Col. Wes ReHorn (Hand guns)

August 20...Greg Bohanan, FLW Pro Fisherman

August 27...Beau Gage, Blind Faith (duck hunter devo)

Sept 3...Alan Bland, Corps of Engineers Beaver Lake

Sept 10... Tron Peterson, Peterson Outdoor Ministry (Joplin, MO)

Sept 17...Matt Tate, Integrated Survival Systems (Part II. Building Shelters)

Sept 24...Tommy Sugg, Cross-country & archery coach at Har-Ber High School

Oct 1...Matt Tate, Integrated Survival Systems (Part III. Finding and purifying food & water)

Oct 8........NO SEVICE THIS DATE

Oct 15...Clay Newcomb, Arkansas Buck & Bears Magazine

Oct 22…Alfred Stevens, Spring Valley Ranch, Long-Range Rifle Fire

OCT 29…JT Harden, Ozarks Outdoors, Joplin, MO

Nov. 5…Jim Greenslade, 3-Rivers Biker Church Mountain Home, AR

Nov 12…Mike Kopeck, Dog Trainer

Nov 19…Buck Ortega, Elk Hunting

Nov 26…NO SERVICE THIS DATE

Dec 3… Manger Build

Dec 10…Manger Build

Dec 17…Pack Rat Outdoor Center (Hiking Gear)

APPENDIX E

JACK'S TOP 10 ADVENTURE BOOKS
Undaunted Courage... by Stephen Ambrose
The Big Sky...by A.B Guthrie, Jr
Wild... by Cheryl Strayed
The Good Life...by Dorian Amos
Hiking Through... by Paul Stutzman
Deliverance...By James Dickey
Braving It... by James Campbell
Endurance...by Alfred Lansing
River Reflections...by Verne Huser
Into Thin Air...By Jon Krakauer

APPENDIX F
"Adventure with a Purpose"

CHAPTER-1... ON THE TRAIL (PERSEVERANCE)
Gal 6:9 "Let us not become weary in doing good, for at the proper time we will reap a harvest if we do not give up."

James 1:12 "Blessed is the one who perseveres under trial because, having stood the test, that person will receive the crown of life that the Lord has promised to those who love him."

CHAPTER-2...PARADISE OUTFITTERS (SPIRITUAL DEVELOPMENT)
Hebrews 5:14 "But solid food is for the mature who by constant use have trained themselves to distinguish good from evil."

James 1:4 "Let perseverance finish its work so that you may be mature and complete, not lacking anything."

CHAPTER-3... BOOT CAMP (CREATING MEMORIES)
Exodus 33:13 "If you are pleased with me, teach me your ways so I may know you and continue to find favor with you. Remember that this nation is your people."

1. Chronicles 16:12 "Remember the wonders he has done, his miracles, and the judgments he pronounced."

CHAPTER-4... THE OUTDOOR CHURCH (IMPACT)

Matthew 5:13 "Jesus said, "You are the salt of the earth; but if the salt loses its flavor, how shall it be seasoned? It is then good for nothing but to be thrown out and trampled underfoot by men."

Matthew 5:14-16 Jesus said that, "You are the light of the world. A city that is set on a hill cannot be hidden. Nor do they light a lamp and put it under a basket, but on a lampstand, and it gives light to all *who are* in the house. Let your light so shine before men, that they may see your good works and glorify your Father in heaven."

CHAPTER-5... PURE ADVENTURE (PASSION)

2. Peter 1:5-7 "Now for this very reason also, applying all diligence, in your faith supply moral excellence, and in your moral excellence, knowledge; 6 and in your knowledge, self-control, and in your self-control, perseverance, and in your perseverance, godliness; 7 and in your godliness, brotherly kindness, and in your brotherly kindness, love."

Colossians 1:23, "continue in the faith, grounded and steadfast, and are not moved away from the hope of the gospel"

CHAPTER-6... LEADERSHIP LESSONS (PROBLEM SOLVER)

Proverbs 3:5 "Trust in the Lord with all your heart, and do not lean on your own understanding."

Joshua 3:1-17 Crossing the Jordan River

CHAPTER-7... DISCOVERY (RISK)

Matthew 14:29 He said, "Come." So Peter got out of the boat and walked on the water and came to Jesus."

2 Timothy 1:7 "For God gave us a spirit not of fear but of power and love and self-control."

CHAPTER-8... DAVID'S ADVENTURES (COURAGE)

1 Samuel 26:5-13 David spares Saul's life

1. Samuel 17:47-50 "David ran quickly to the battle line to meet the Philistine. David put his hand in the bag, took out a stone, slung it, and hit the Philistine on his forehead. The stone sank into his forehead, and he fell on his face to the ground. David defeated the Philistine with a sling and a stone."

CHAPTER-9... EXPEDITIONARY MEN (FREEDOM)

Gal. 5:1 "For freedom Christ has set us free; stand firm therefore, and do not submit again to a yoke of slavery."

Roman 8:21 "That the creation itself will be set free from its bondage to corruption and obtain the freedom of the glory of the children of God."

CHAPTER-10... ACT LIKE MEN (VIGILANCE)

2 Chronicles 7:14 "Be alert, stand firm in the faith, act like, men, be strong."

1. Peter 5:8 "Be sober-minded; be watchful. Your adversary the devil prowls around like a roaring lion, seeking someone to devour."

CHAPTER-11...THE MAP (DIRECTION)

Psalm 32:8 "I will instruct you and teach you in the way you should go; I will counsel you with my eye upon you."

Psalm 119:105 "Your word is a lamp for my feet and a light on my path."

CHAPTER-12... NEXT STEPS (CHALLENGE)

Jeremiah 29:11 "For I know the plans I have for you, declares the Lord, plans for welfare and not for evil, to give you a future and a hope."

Matthew 28:19 "Go therefore and make disciples of all nations, baptizing them in the name of the Father and of the Son and of the Holy Spirit."

Job 42:12 "So the LORD blessed the last part of Job's life more than the first..."

APPENDIX G

APPENDIX H
Trail Map

Nazareth to Capernaum

Click points of interest to explore

Mt. of Beatitudes
Tabgha
Capernaum
St. Peter's Primacy
Migdal
Ginosar
Nebi Shu'eib
Arbel
Horns of Hattin
Lavi
Sea of Galilee
Tiberias
Zippori
Cana
Ilaniya
Mashhad
Nazareth
Mt. Precipice
Mt. Tabor
Jordan River
JesusTrail.com